Congressional Investigations of the Department of Justice, 1920-2007: History, Law, and Practice. Indexed

Congressional Investigations of the Department of Justice, 1920-2007: History, Law, and Practice. Indexed

Morton Rosenberg

Nova Science Publishers, Inc.
New York

For permission to use material from this book please contact us:
Telephone 631-231-7269; Fax 631-231-8175
Web Site: http://www.novapublishers.com

LIBRARY OF CONGRESS CATALOGING-IN-PUBLICATION DATA

Rosenberg, Morton, 1935-

Congressional investigations of the Department of Justice, 1920-2007 : history, law, and practice. Indexed / Morton Rosenbergá (Author).

p. cm.

Includes bibliographical references and index.

ISBN 978-1-60456-194-4 (hardcover : alk. paper)

1. United States. Dept. of Justice--History. 2. Governmental investigations--United States. 3. Justice, Administration of--United States--History. I. Title.

KF5107.R67 2007

347.73--dc22 *2007044745*

Published by Nova Science Publishers, Inc. ✣ New York

Contents

Preface		**vii**
Chapter 1	Introduction	**1**
Chapter 2	The Legal Basis for Oversight	**5**
Chapter 3	Illustrative Investigations and Case Law	**9**
	Teapot Dome	**10**
	Burford I: The Superfund Investigation	**11**
	Burford II: The Investigation of the Claim of Presidential Privilege	**12**
	Rocky Flats	**16**
	Corruption in the FBI's Boston Regional Office	**17**
	Ruby Ridge	**19**
Chapter 4	Assessment of DOJ's Opposition to Congressional Access to Information in Open and Closed Litigation Files and to Internal Deliberative Materials	**23**
	The Department's Position	**23**
	Assessment of the Department's Position	**24**
Chapter 5	Concluding Observations	**39**
Appendix.	Selected Congressional Investigations of the Department of Justice, 1920-2007	**43**
	Palmer Raids	**43**
	Teapot Dome	**44**
	Investigations of DOJ During the 1950's	**46**
	Investigation of Consent Decree Program	**49**

Cointelpro and Related Investigations of FBI-DOJ Misconduct **51**
White Collar Crime in the Oil Industry **53**
Billy Carter/Libya Investigation **54**
Undercover Law Enforcement Activities (ABSCAM) **55**
Investigation of Withholding of EPA Documents **58**
E.F. Hutton Investigation **62**
Iran-Contra **63**
Rocky Flats Environmental Crimes Plea Bargain **64**
Investigation of the Justice Department's Environmental Crimes Section **66**
Campaign Finance Investigations **68**
Misuse of Informants in the FBI's Boston Regional Office **70**
Removal and Replacement of United States Attorneys **72**

References **75**

Index **83**

PREFACE

The rich history of congressional investigations from the failed St. Clair expedition in 1792 through Teapot Dome, Watergate, Iran-Contra, Whitewater, and the current ongoing inquiries into the removal and replacement of United States Attorneys, has established, in law and practice, the nature and contours of congressional prerogatives necessary to maintain the integrity of the legislative role in that constitutional scheme. A review of the historical experience and legal rulings pertinent to congressional access to information regarding the law enforcement activities of the Department of Justice indicates that in the last 85 years Congress has consistently sought and obtained deliberative prosecutorial memoranda, and the testimony of line attorneys, FBI field agents and other subordinate agency employees regarding the conduct of open and closed cases in the course of innumerable investigations of Department of Justice activities.

Legislative oversight is most commonly conducted through congressional budget, authorization, appropriations, confirmation, and investigative processes, and, in rare instances, through impeachment. But the adversarial, often confrontational, and sometimes high profile nature of congressional investigations sets it apart from the more routine, accommodative facets of the oversight process experienced in authorization, appropriations, or confirmation exercises. While all aspects of legislative oversight share the common goals of informing Congress so as to best accomplish its tasks of developing legislation, monitoring the implementation of public policy, and disclosing to the public how its government is performing, the inquisitorial process also sustains and vindicates Congress' role in our constitutional scheme of separated powers and checks and balances.

These investigations have encompassed virtually every component of the DOJ and its officials and employees, from the Attorney General down to subordinate level personnel. It appears that the fact that an agency, such as the Justice Department, has determined for its own internal purposes that a particular item should not be disclosed, or that the information sought should come from one agency source rather than another, does not prevent either House of Congress, or its committees or subcommittees, from obtaining and publishing information it considers essential for the proper performance of its constitutional functions. There appears to be no court precedent that imposes a threshold burden on committees to demonstrate, for example, a "substantial reason to believe wrongdoing occurred" before a jurisdictional committee may seek disclosure with respect to the conduct of specific open and closed criminal and civil cases. Indeed, the case law is quite to the contrary. An inquiring committee need only show that the information sought is within the broad subject matter of its authorized jurisdiction, is in aid of a legitimate legislative function, and is pertinent to the area of concern. Moreover, there have been only two formal presidential assertions of executive privilege with respect to withholding of internal DOJ documents in the face of a congressional subpoena. Those claims were ultimately abandoned, and it appears under the most recent Supreme Court and appellate court rulings pertinent to the scope of the presidential communications privilege and the "Take Care" clause of the Constitution, that such a claim would be open to serious question as to its validity in the context of a congressional probe of DOJ internal deliberative actions.

Chapter 1

INTRODUCTION

Throughout its history, Congress has engaged in oversight of the executive branch — the review, monitoring, and supervision of the implementation of public policy. The first several Congresses inaugurated such important oversight techniques as special investigations, reporting requirements, resolutions of inquiry, and use of the appropriations process to review executive activity. Contemporary developments, moreover, have increased the legislature's capacity and capabilities to check on and check the executive. Public laws and congressional rules have measurably enhanced Congress's implied power under the Constitution to conduct oversight.[1]

Congressional oversight of the executive is designed to fulfill a number of important purposes and goals: to ensure executive compliance with legislative intent; to improve the efficiency, effectiveness, and economy of governmental operations; to evaluate program performance; to prevent executive encroachment on legislative powers and prerogatives; to investigate alleged instances of poor administration, arbitrary and capricious behavior, abuse, waste, fraud and dishonesty; to assess agency or officials' ability to manage and carry out program objectives; to assess the need for new federal legislation; to review and determine federal financial priorities; to protect individual rights and liberties; and to inform the public as to the manner in which its government is performing its public duties, among others.[2]

Legislative oversight is most commonly conducted through congressional budget, authorization, appropriations, confirmation, and investigative processes, and, in rare instances, through impeachment. But the adversarial, often confrontational, and sometimes high profile nature of congressional investigations sets it apart from the more routine, accommodative facets of the oversight process experienced in authorization, appropriations, or confirmation exercises. While all aspects of legislative oversight share the common goals of informing Congress so as to best accomplish its tasks of developing legislation, monitoring the implementation of public policy, and of disclosing to the public how its government is performing, the inquisitorial process also sustains and vindicates Congress' role in our constitutional scheme of separated powers and checks and balances. The rich history of congressional investigations from the failed St. Clair expedition in 1792 through Teapot Dome, Watergate, Iran-Contra, Whitewater, and the current ongoing inquiries into the removal and replacement of United States Attorneys, has established, in law and practice, the nature and contours of congressional prerogatives necessary to maintain the integrity of the legislative role in that constitutional scheme.

Congress' power of inquiry extends to all executive departments, agencies, and establishments in equal measure. Over time, however, congressional probes of the Department of Justice (Department or DOJ) have proved to be amongst the most contentious, stemming from the presumptive sensitivity of its principal law enforcement mission. Often, inquiries have been met with claims of improper political interference with discretionary deliberative prosecutorial processes, accompanied by refusals to supply internal documents or testimony sought by jurisdictional committees, based on assertions of constitutional and common law privileges or general statutory exemptions from disclosure. But the notion of, and need for, protection of the internal deliberative processes of agency policymaking, heightened sensitivity to premature disclosures of decisionmaking involving law enforcement investigations, civil and criminal prosecutions, or security matters, is not unique to the DOJ, though the degree of day-to-day involvement there with such matters may be greater. An in-depth examination of the nature, scope, and resolution of such past investigative confrontations with the DOJ appears useful for informing future committees determining whether to undertake similar probes of DOJ, or other executive agencies, as to the scope and limits of their investigative prerogatives and the practical problems of such undertakings.

A review of the historical experience and legal rulings pertinent to congressional access to information regarding the law enforcement activities of the Department of Justice indicates that in the last 85 years Congress has consistently sought and obtained deliberative prosecutorial memoranda, and the testimony of line attorneys, FBI field agents and other subordinate agency employees regarding the conduct of open and closed cases in the course of innumerable investigations of Department of Justice activities. These investigations have encompassed virtually every component of the DOJ, and all officials, and employees, from the Attorney General down to subordinate level personnel. It appears that the fact that an agency, such as the Justice Department, has determined for its own internal purposes that a particular item should not be disclosed, or that the information sought should come from one agency source rather than another, does not prevent either House of Congress, or its committees or subcommittees, from obtaining and publishing information it considers essential for the proper performance of its constitutional functions. There appears to be no court precedent that imposes a threshold burden on committees to demonstrate, for example, a "substantial reason to believe wrongdoing occurred" before a jurisdictional committee may seek disclosure with respect to the conduct of specific open and closed criminal and civil cases. Indeed, the case law is quite to the contrary. An inquiring committee need only show that the information sought is within the broad subject matter of its authorized jurisdiction, is in aid of a legitimate legislative function, and is pertinent to the area of concern. Moreover, there have been only two formal presidential assertions of executive privilege with respect to withholding of internal DOJ documents in the face of a congressional subpoena.[3] Those claims were ultimately abandoned, and it appears under the most recent Supreme Court and appellate court rulings pertinent to the scope of the presidential communications privilege and the "Take Care" clause of the constitution, that such a claim would be open to serious question as to its validity in the context of a congressional probe of DOJ internal deliberative actions.

Committees, however, normally have been restrained by prudential considerations that involve a pragmatic assessment informed by weighing consideration of legislative need, public policy, and the statutory duty of congressional committees to engage in continuous oversight of the application, administration and execution of laws that fall within their jurisdiction, against the potential burdens and harms that may be imposed on an agency if deliberative process matter is publically disclosed. In particular, sensitive law enforcement concerns and duties of the Justice Department have been seen to merit that substantial weight be given the agency's deliberative processes in the absence of a reasonable belief of a jurisdictional committee that government misconduct has occurred. A careful review of the historical record indicates a generally faithful congressional adherence to these prudential considerations.

The discussion will proceed as follows. The legal basis for investigative oversight will be briefly reviewed, followed by several prominent examples of congressional oversight that reflect significant milestones in the establishment of the breadth and reach of the legislative investigative prerogative vis-a-vis the Department. Next we will review and assess the Department's contentions, based on policy and common law and constitutional privilege, that it has asserted to attempt to limit congressional access to agency information. An appendix to this report provides summaries of 18 inquiries in which committees have successfully obtained documents and testimony respecting the internal deliberative processes involving open and closed civil and criminal cases, as well as programmatic matters that are part of the Department's statutory mission.

Chapter 2

THE LEGAL BASIS FOR OVERSIGHT

Numerous Supreme Court precedents recognize a broad and encompassing power in Congress to engage in oversight and investigation that would reach all sources of information necessary for carrying out its legislative function. In the absence of a countervailing constitutional privilege or a self-imposed statutory restriction upon its authority, Congress and its committees have virtually plenary power to compel production of information needed to discharge their legislative functions from executive agencies, private persons, and organizations. Within certain constraints, the information so obtained may be made public.

Although there is no express provision of the Constitution that specifically authorizes Congress to conduct investigations and take testimony for the purposes of performing its legitimate functions, numerous decisions of the Supreme Court have firmly established that the investigatory power of Congress is so essential to the legislative function as to be implied from the general vesting of legislative power in Congress.[4] Thus, in *Eastland v. United States Servicemen's Fund*, the Court explained that "[t]he scope of its power of inquiry ... is as penetrating and far-reaching as the potential power to enact and appropriate under the Constitution."[5] In *Watkins v. United States,* the Court described the breadth of the power of inquiry: "The power of the Congress to conduct investigations is inherent in the legislative process. That power is broad. It encompasses inquiries concerning the administration of existing laws as well as proposed or possibly needed statutes."[6] The Court went on to emphasize that Congress's investigative power is at its peak when the subject is alleged waste, fraud, abuse, or maladministration within a government department. The investigative power, it stated, "comprehends probes into departments of the Federal Government to expose corruption, inefficiency, or waste."[7] "[T]he first Congresses," it continued, held "inquiries dealing with suspected corruption or mismanagement of government officials"[8] and subsequently, in a series of decisions, "[t]he court recognized the danger to effective and honest conduct of the Government if the legislative power to probe corruption in the Executive Branch were unduly hampered."[9] Accordingly, the Court stated, it recognizes "the power of the Congress to inquire into and publicize corruption, maladministration, or inefficiencies in the agencies of Government."[10]

The breadth of a jurisdictional committee's investigative authority may be seen in the two seminal Supreme Court decisions emanating from the Teapot Dome inquiries of the mid-1920's, both involving, directly and indirectly, the Department of Justice. As part of its investigation, the Senate select committee issued a subpoena for the testimony of Mally S. Daugherty, the brother of the Attorney General. After Daugherty failed to respond to the subpoena, the Senate sent its Deputy Sergeant at Arms to take him into custody and bring him before the Senate. Daugherty petitioned in federal court for a writ of *habeas corpus* arguing that the Senate in its investigation had exceeded its constitutional powers. The case ultimately reached the Supreme Court, where, in a landmark decision, *McGrain v. Daugherty,[11]* the Court upheld the Senate's authority to investigate charges concerning the Department:

> [T]he subject to be investigated was the administration of the Department of Justice - whether its functions were being properly discharged or were being neglected or misdirected, and particularly whether the Attorney General and his assistants were performing or neglecting their duties in respect of the institution and prosecution of proceedings to punish crimes and enforce appropriate remedies against the wrongdoers - specific instances of alleged neglect being recited. Plainly the subject was one on which legislation could be had and would be materially aided by the information which the investigation was calculated to elicit. This becomes manifest when it is reflected that the functions of the Department of Justice, the powers and duties of the Attorney General and the duties of his assistants, are all subject to congressional legislation, and that the department is maintained and its activities are carried on under such appropriations as in the judgment of Congress are needed from year to year.[12]

The Court thus underlined that the Department of Justice, like all other executive departments and agencies, is a creature of the Congress and subject to its plenary legislative and oversight authority.

In another Teapot Dome case that reached the Supreme Court, *Sinclair v. United States,[13]* a different witness at the congressional hearings refused to provide answers, and was prosecuted for contempt of Congress. The witness had noted that a lawsuit had been commenced between the government and the Mammoth Oil Company, and declared, "I shall reserve any evidence I may be able to give for those courts... and shall respectfully decline to answer any questions propounded by your committee."[14] The Supreme Court upheld the witness' conviction for contempt of Congress. The Court considered and rejected in unequivocal terms the witness' contention that the pendency of lawsuits provided an excuse for withholding information. Neither the laws directing that such lawsuits be instituted, nor the lawsuits themselves, "operated to divest the Senate, or the committee, of power further to investigate the actual administration of the land laws."[15] The Court further explained: "It may be conceded that Congress is without authority to compel disclosure for the purpose of aiding the prosecution of pending suits; but the authority of that body, directly or through its committees to require pertinent disclosures in aid of its own constitutional power is not abridged because the information sought to be elicited may also be of use in such suits."[16] The *Sinclair* ruling inferentially indicates that the Department's oft-proffered distinction between open and closed cases has little weight.

Chapter 3

ILLUSTRATIVE INVESTIGATIONS AND CASE LAW

Perhaps most instructive and illuminating for present purposes is a review of important precedents over the last 85 years regarding oversight of the Justice Department. Appended to this report are brief summaries of 18 selected congressional investigations from the Palmer Raids and Teapot Dome in the 1920's to Watergate and through Iran-Contra, Rocky Flats, corruption in the FBI's Boston regional office, and the recent inquiries into the termination and replacement of United States Attorneys. Those investigations demonstrate that DOJ has consistently been obligated to submit to congressional oversight, regardless of whether litigation is pending or is anticipated, so that Congress is not delayed unduly in investigating maladministration, misfeasance and/or malfeasance in the Justice Department and elsewhere. A number of these investigations spawned seminal Supreme Court rulings that today provide the foundation for the broad congressional power of inquiry. All were contentious and involved Department claims that committee demands for agency documents and testimony were precluded either on the basis of constitutional or common law privilege or policy. In the majority of instances reviewed, the testimony of subordinate DOJ employees, such as line attorneys and FBI field agents, was taken formally or informally, and included detailed testimony about specific instances of the Department's failure to prosecute alleged meritorious cases. In all instances, investigating committees were provided with documents respecting open or closed cases that often included prosecutorial memoranda, FBI investigative reports, summaries of FBI interviews, memoranda and correspondence prepared during the pendency of cases, confidential instructions outlining the procedures or guidelines to be followed for undercover operations and the surveillance and arrest of subjects, and documents presented to grand juries not protected from disclosure by Rule 6(e) of the Federal Rules of Criminal Procedure, among other similar "sensitive" materials. The instances of DOJ oversight reviewed of course are not exhaustive of such inquiries. The consequences of these historic inquiries at times have been profound and far reaching, directly leading to important remedial legislation and the resignations (Harry M. Daugherty, J. Howard McGrath, Alberto R. Gonzales) and convictions (Richard Kleidienst, John Mitchell) of five attorneys general.

TEAPOT DOME

The Teapot Dome scandal in the mid-1920's provided the model and indisputable authority for wide ranging congressional inquiries. While the Senate Committee on Public Lands and Surveys focused on the actions of the Department of the Interior in leasing naval oil reserves, a Senate select committee was constituted to investigate "charges of misfeasance and nonfeasance in the Department of Justice"[17] in failing to prosecute the malefactors in the Department of the Interior, as well as other cases.[18] The select committee heard from scores of present and former attorneys and agents of the Department and its Bureau of Investigation, who offered detailed testimony about specific instances of the Department's failure to prosecute alleged meritorious cases. Not all of the cases upon which testimony was offered were closed, as one of the committee's goals in its questioning was to identify cases in which the statute of limitations had not run out and prosecution was still possible.[19]

The committee also obtained access to Department documentation, including prosecutorial memoranda on a wide range of matters. However, given the charges of widespread corruption in the Department and the imminent resignation of Attorney General Daugherty, it would appear that some of the documents furnished the committee early in the hearings may have been volunteered by the witnesses and not officially provided by the Department. Although Attorney General Daugherty had promised cooperation with the committee, and had agreed to provide access to at least the files of closed cases,[20] such cooperation apparently had not been forthcoming.[21]

In two instances immediately following Daugherty's resignation, the committee was refused access to confidential Bureau of Investigation investigative reports pending the appointment of a new Attorney General who could advise the President about such production,[22] though witnesses from the Department were permitted to testify about the investigations that were the subject of the investigative reports and even to read at the hearings from the investigative reports. With the appointment of the new Attorney General, Harlan F. Stone, the committee was granted broad access to Department files. Committee Chairman Smith Brookhard remarked that "[Stone] is furnishing us with all the files we want, whereas the former Attorney General, Mr. Daugherty, refused nearly all that we asked."[23] For example, with the authorization of the new Attorney General, an accountant with the Department who had led an investigation of fraudulent sales of property by the Alien Property Custodian's office appeared and produced his confidential reports to the Bureau of Investigation. The reports described the factual findings from his investigation and his recommendations for further action, and included the names of companies and individuals suspected of making false claims. The Department had not acted on those recommendations, though the cases had not been closed.[24] A similar investigative report, concerning an inquiry into the disappearance of large quantities of liquor under the control of the Department during the prior administration of President Harding, was also produced.[25]

BURFORD I: THE SUPERFUND INVESTIGATION

In 1982, during the second session of the 97th Congress, the House Transportation Committee's Public Works Subcommittee on Oversight and the House Energy and Commerce's Subcommittee on Oversight and Investigations initiated investigations of the Environmental Protection Agency's (EPA) enforcement of the "Superfund" law.[26] The committees requested documents relating to a number of on-going enforcement investigations from EPA Administrator Anne Gorsuch Burford. The documents sought included memoranda of EPA and DOJ attorneys containing litigation and negotiation strategy, settlement positions, and other similar materials.[27] After Ms. Burford's initial refusal, the subcommittees issued subpoenas but compliance was resisted on the grounds that the documents requested were "enforcement sensitive"and were to be found in open law enforcement files. At the direction of President Reagan, Ms. Burford claimed executive privilege to prevent their disclosure.

The House Transportation Subcommittee acted first, citing Ms. Burford for contempt of Congress, an action that was affirmed by the full Committee.

The full House of Representatives voted 259 to 105 to support the contempt citation.[28] After the DOJ's failed attempt at obtaining a federal court order enjoining the House from forwarding the contempt citation to the U.S. Attorney for prosecution pursuant to the criminal contempt statute,[29] and following a brief period of negotiation with the Public Works and Transportation Committee, it was agreed that the documents would be released to the subcommittee in stages, beginning first with briefings and redacted copies, and eventually ending with unredacted copies that could only be examined by committee members and up to two designated committee staffers.[30]

The Chairman of the House Energy and Commerce Committee, Representative John Dingell, refused to accept the agreement between the DOJ and the House Public Works and Transportation Committee given its limitations on access and time delays. After a threat to issue new subpoenas and pursue a further contempt citation, negotiations were resumed. The result was an agreement that all documents covered by the initial subpoena were to be delivered to the subcommittee. There were to be no briefings and no multi-stage process of redacted documents leading to unredacted documents.[31] The subcommittee agreed to handle all "enforcement sensitive" documents in executive session, giving them confidential treatment.[32] The subcommittee, however, reserved for itself the right to release the documents or use them in public session, after providing "reasonable notice" to the EPA.[33] If the EPA did not agree, the documents would not be released or used in public session unless the Chairman and Ranking Minority Member concurred.[34] If they did not concur, the subcommittee could vote on the release of documents and their subsequent use in a public session.[35] Staff access was to be decided by the Chairman and Ranking Minority Member.[36] The agreement was signed by Chairman Dingell, Ranking Member James T. Broyhill, and White House Counsel Fred F. Fielding on March 9, 1983.[37] The ultimate agreement is an illustration of the autonomy of jurisdictional committees in the House of Representatives.

BURFORD II: THE INVESTIGATION OF THE CLAIM OF PRESIDENTIAL PRIVILEGE

After committee access to the Superfund enforcement documents was obtained, a number of questions about the role of the Department during the controversy remained: whether the Department, not EPA, had made the decision to persuade the President to assert executive privilege; whether the Department had directed the United States Attorney for the District of Columbia not to present the contempt certification of Burford to the grand jury for prosecution and had made the decision to sue the House; and, generally, whether there was a conflict of interest in the Department's simultaneously advising the President, representing Burford, investigating alleged Executive branch wrongdoing, and enforcing the congressional criminal contempt statute. These and related questions raised by the Department's actions were the subject of an investigation by the House Judiciary Committee beginning in early 1983. The committee issued a final report on its investigation in December 1985.[38]

Although the Judiciary Committee ultimately was able to obtain access to virtually all of the documentation and other information it sought from the Department, in many respects this investigation proved as contentious as the earlier EPA controversy from which it arose. In its final report, the committee concluded that:

> [T]he Department of Justice, through many of the same senior officials who were most involved in the EPA controversy, consciously prevented the Judiciary Committee from obtaining information in the Department's possession that was essential to the Committee's inquiry into the Department's role in that controversy. Most notably, the Department deliberately, and without advising the Committee, withheld a massive volume of vital handwritten notes and chronologies for over one year. These materials, which the Department knew came within the Committee's February 1983 document request, contained the bulk of the relevant documentary information about the Department's activities outlined in this report and provided a basis for many of the Committee's findings.[39]

Among the other abuses cited by the committee were the withholding of a number of relevant documents until the committee had independently learned of their existence,[40] as well as materially "false and misleading" testimony before the committee by the head of the Department's Office of Legal Counsel.[41]

The committee's initial request for documentation was contained in a February 1983 letter from its chairman, Peter Rodino, to Attorney General William French Smith. The committee requested the Department to "supply all documents prepared by or in the possession of the Department in any way relating to the withholding of documents that Congressional committees have subpoenaed from the EPA."[42] The letter also specifically requested, among other things, a narrative description of the activities of each division or other unit of the Department relating to the withholding of the EPA materials, information about the Department's apparent conflict of interest in simultaneously advising the Executive Branch while being responsible for prosecuting the Burford contempt citation, and any instructions given by the Department to the United States Attorney for the District of Columbia not to present the Burford contempt to the grand jury.

At first the Department provided only publicly available documents in response to this and other document requests of the committee.[43] However, after a series of meetings between committee staff and senior Department officials, an agreement was reached whereby committee staff were permitted to review the materials responsive to these requests at the Department to determine which documents the committee would need for its inquiry.[44] Committee staff reviewed thousands of documents from the Land and Natural Resources Division, the Civil Division, the Office of Legal Counsel, the Office of Legislative Affairs, the Office of Public Affairs, and the offices of the Attorney General, the Deputy Attorney General, and the Solicitor General.[45]

In July 1983, the committee chairman wrote to the Attorney General requesting copies of 105 documents that committee staff had identified in its review as particularly important to the committee's inquiry.[46] By May 1984, only a few of those documents had been provided to the committee, and the chairman again wrote to the Attorney General requesting the Department's cooperation in the investigation. In that letter, the chairman advised the Attorney General that the committee's preliminary investigation had raised serious questions of misconduct, including potential criminal misconduct, in the actions of the Department in the withholding of the EPA documents.[47] The committee finally received all of the 105 documents in July 1984, a full year after it had initially requested access. The committee at that time also obtained the written notes and a number of other documents that had been earlier withheld.[48]

There was also disagreement about the access that would be provided to Department employees for interviews with committee staff. The Department demanded that it be permitted to have one or more Department attorneys present at each interview. The committee feared that the presence of Department representatives might intimidate the Department employees in their interviews and stated that it was willing to permit a Department representative to be present only if the representative was "walled-off" from Department officials involved with the controversy, if the substance of interviews was not revealed to subsequent interviewees, and if employees could be interviewed without a Department representative present if so requested. The Department ultimately agreed to permit the interviews to go forward without its attorneys present. If a Department employee requested representation, the Department employed private counsel for that purpose. In all, committee staff interviewed twenty-six current and former Department employees, including four Assistant Attorney Generals, under this agreement.[49]

Partly as a result of these interviews, as well as from information in the handwritten notes that had been initially withheld, the committee concluded that it also required access to Criminal Division documents concerning the origins of the criminal investigation of former EPA Assistant Administrator Rita Lavelle in order to determine if the Department had considered instituting the investigation to obstruct the committee's inquiry. The committee also requested information about the Department's earlier withholding of the handwritten notes and other documents to determine whether Department officials had deliberately withheld the documents in an attempt to obstruct the committee's investigation.[50] The Department at first refused to provide the committee with documents relating to its Lavelle investigation "[c]onsistent with the longstanding practice of the Department not to provide access to active criminal files."[51] The Department also refused to provide the committee with access to documentation related to the Department's handling of the committee's inquiry, objecting to the committee's "ever- broadening scope of ...inquiry."[52]

The committee chairman wrote the Attorney General and objected that the Department was denying the committee access even though no claim of executive privilege had been asserted.[53] The chairman also maintained that "[i]n this case, of course, no claim of executive privilege could lie because of the interest of the committee in determining whether the documents contain evidence of misconduct by executive branch officials."[54] With respect to the documents relating to the Department's handling of the committee inquiry, the chairman demanded that the Department prepare a detailed index of the withheld documents, including the title, date, and length of each document, its author and all who had seen it, a summary of its contents, an explanation of why it was being withheld, and a certification that the Department intended to recommend to the President the assertion of executive privilege as to each withheld document and that each document contained no evidence of misconduct.[55] With respect to the Lavelle documents, the chairman narrowed the committee's request to "predicate" documents relating to the opening of the investigation and prosecution of Lavelle, as opposed to FBI and other investigative reports reflecting actual investigative work conducted after the opening of the investigation.[56] In response, after a period of more than three months from the committee's initial request, the Department produced those two categories of materials.[57]

ROCKY FLATS

Another revealing investigation involved a 1992 inquiry of the Subcommittee on Investigations and Oversight of the House Committee on Science, Space, and Technology which commenced a review of the plea bargain settlement by the Department of Justice of the government's investigation and prosecution of environmental crimes committed by Rockwell International Corporation in its capacity as manager and operating contractor at the Department of Energy's (DOE) Rocky Flats nuclear weapons facility.[58] The settlement was a culmination of a five-year investigation of environmental crimes at the facility, conducted by a joint government task force involving the FBI, the Department of Justice, the Environmental Protection Agency (EPA), EPA's National Enforcement Investigation Centers, and the DOE Inspector General. The subcommittee was concerned with the size of the fine agreed to relative to the profits made by the contractor and the damage caused by inappropriate activities; the lack of personal indictments of either Rockwell or DOE personnel despite a DOJ finding that the crimes were "institutional crimes" that "were the result of a culture, substantially encouraged and nurtured by DOE, where environmental compliance was a much lower priority than the production and recovery of plutonium and the manufacture of nuclear 'triggers'"; and that reimbursements provided by the government to Rockwell for expenses in the cases and the contractual arrangements between Rockwell and DOE may have created disincentives for environmental compliance and aggressive prosecution of the case.

The subcommittee held ten days of hearings, seven in executive session, in which it took testimony from the United States Attorney for the District of Colorado; an assistant U.S. Attorney for the District of Colorado; a DOJ line attorney from Main Justice; and an FBI field agent; and received voluminous FBI field investigative reports and interview summaries, and documents submitted to the grand jury not subject to Rule 6(e).[59]

At one point in the proceedings, however, all the witnesses who were under subpoena, upon written instructions from the Acting Assistant Attorney General, Criminal Division, refused to answer questions concerning internal deliberations in which decisions were made about the investigation and prosecution of Rockwell, the DOE and their employees. Two of the witnesses advised that they had information and, but for the DOJ directive, would have answered the subcommittee's inquiries. The subcommittee members unanimously authorized the chairman to send a letter to President Bush requesting that he either personally assert executive privilege as the basis for directing the witnesses to withhold the information or direct DOJ to retract its instructions to the witnesses. The President took neither course and the DOJ subsequently reiterated its position that the matter sought would chill Department personnel. The subcommittee then moved to hold the U .S. Attorney in contempt of Congress.

A last minute agreement forestalled the contempt citation. Under the agreement (1) DOJ issued a new instruction to all personnel under subpoena to answer all questions put to them by the subcommittee, including those which related to internal deliberations with respect to the plea bargain. Those instructions were to apply as well to all Department witnesses, including FBI personnel, who might be called in the future. Those witnesses were to be advised to answer all questions fully and truthfully and specifically instructed that they were allowed to disclose internal advice, opinions, or recommendations connected to the matter. (2) Transcripts were to be made of all interviews and provided to the witnesses. They were not to be made public except to the extent they needed to be used to refresh the recollection or impeach the testimony of other witnesses called before the subcommittee in a public hearing. (3) Witnesses were to be interviewed by staff under oath. (4) The subcommittee reserved the right to hold further hearings in the future at which time it could call other Department witnesses who would be instructed by the Department not to invoke the deliberative process privilege as a reason for not answering subcommittee questions.[60]

CORRUPTION IN THE FBI'S BOSTON REGIONAL OFFICE

The most recent and definitive exploration and resolution of the question of the nature and breadth of Congress' oversight prerogative with respect to DOJ operations occurred as a consequence of the President's December 2001 claim of executive privilege in response to a subpoena by the House Government Reform Committee. That subpoena sought, among other material, Justice Department documents relating to alleged law enforcement corruption in the Federal Bureau of Investigation's Boston office that occurred over a period of almost 30 years. During that time, FBI officials allegedly knowingly allowed innocent persons to be convicted of murder on the false testimony of a cooperating witness and two informants in order to protect the undercover activities of those informants. Thereafter, Regional Office agents knowingly permitted two other informants to commit some 21 additional murders during the period they acted as informants, and, finally, gave the informants warning of an impending grand jury indictment which allowed one of them to flee. The President directed the Attorney General not to release relevant documents because disclosure "would inhibit the candor necessary to the effectiveness of the deliberative processes by which the Department makes prosecutorial decisions," and that committee access to the documents "threatens to politicize the criminal justice process" and to undermine the fundamental purpose of the separation of power doctrine, "which was to protect individual liberty." In defending the assertion of the privilege the Justice Department claimed a historical policy of withholding deliberative prosecutorial documents from Congress in both open and closed civil and criminal cases.[61] Pending at the time were a number of Federal Tort Claims Act suits brought by the convicted persons and their families, alleging that the government was aware of and knowingly allowed the false testimony.

Initial congressional hearings after the claim was made demonstrated the rigidity of the Department's position. The Department later agreed there might be some area for compromise, and on January 10, 2002, White House Counsel Alberto Gonzales wrote to Chairman Burton conceding that it was a "misimpression" that congressional committees could never have access to deliberative documents from a criminal investigation or prosecution. "There is no such bright-line policy, nor did we intend to articulate any such policy." But, he continued, since the documents "sought a very narrow and particularly sensitive category of deliberative matters" and "absent unusual circumstances, the Executive Branch has traditionally protected these highly sensitive deliberative documents against public or congressional disclosure" unless a committee showed a "compelling or specific need" for the documents.[62] The documents continued to be withheld until a further hearing, held on February 6, 2002, when the committee heard expert testimony describing over 30 specific instances since 1920 of the Department of Justice allowing congressional access to prosecutorial memoranda for both open and closed cases and providing testimony of subordinate Department employees, such as line attorneys, FBI field agents and U.S. attorneys, and included detailed testimony about specific instances of DOJ's failure to prosecute meritorious cases. In all the described instances, investigating committees were provided with documents respecting open and closed cases that often included prosecutorial memoranda, FBI investigative reports, summaries of FBI interviews, memoranda and correspondence prepared during undercover operations, and documents presented to grand juries not protected by Rule 6(e), among other similar "sensitive materials." Shortly after the hearing the committee was given access to the disputed documents.[63]

The committee's final report concluded that the documents withheld from it were indispensable to its inquiry and that the claim of presidential privilege was part of a pattern of obstruction that impeded its investigation:

> When the FBI Office of Professional Responsibility conducted an investigation of the activities of New England law enforcement, it concluded in 1997: "There is no evidence that prosecutorial discretion was exercised on behalf of informants [James] Bulger and/or [Stephen] Flemmi." This is untrue. Former U.S. Attorney Jeremiah O'Sullivan was asked in the December 5, 2002 Committee hearing whether prosecutorial discretion had been exercised on behalf of Bulger and Flemmi and he said that it had. A review of documents in the possession of the Justice Department also confirms this to be true. Had thecommittee permitted the assertion of executive privilege by the President to be unchallenged, this information would never have been known. That the Justice Department concluded that prosecutorial discretion had not benefitted Bulger or Flemmi — while at the same time fighting to keep Congress from obtaining information proving this statement to be untrue — is extremely troubling.[64]

RUBY RIDGE

The instances of successful committee access to DOJ documents and witnesses related in the above discussed inquiries (as well as those detailed in the Appendix to this report) encompassed a wide number of divisions, bureaus, and offices at Main Justice and U.S. Attorneys offices in the field, and involved the Department's politically sensitive Public Integrity Section,[65] and provide a substantial basis for arguing that no element of the DOJ is exempt from oversight by a jurisdictional committee of the Congress. One additional case study, involving the DOJ Office of Professional Responsibility, which monitors the conduct of Department personnel, is notable for its revelations of a number of sensitive, undisclosed internal investigations in the face of extraordinary agency resistance. That occurred during the 1995 investigation by the Senate Judiciary Committee's Subcommittee on Terrorism, Technology and Government Information of allegations that several branches of the Department of Justice and the Department of the Treasury had engaged in serious criminal and professional misconduct in the investigation, apprehension, and prosecution of Randall Weaver and Kevin Harris at Ruby Ridge, Idaho. The subcommittee held 14 days of hearings in which it heard testimony from 62 witnesses, including Justice, Federal Bureau of Investigation, and Treasury officials, line attorneys and agents, and obtained various Justice, FBI and Treasury internal reports,[66] and issued a final report.[67]

The subcommittee's hearings revealed that the involved federal agencies conducted at least eight internal investigations into charges of misconduct at Ruby Ridge, none of which had ever been publically released.[68] DOJ expressed reluctance to allow the Subcommittee to see the documents out of a concern they would interfere with the ongoing investigation but ultimately provided some of them under conditions with respect to their public release. The most important of those documents was the Report of the Ruby Ridge Task Force.[69] The Task Force was established by the DOJ after the acquittals of Randy Weaver and Kevin Harris of all charges in the killing of a Deputy United States Marshal[70] to investigate charges that federal law enforcement agents and federal prosecutors involved in the investigation, apprehension and prosecution of Weaver and Harris may have engaged in professional misconduct and criminal wrongdoing. The allegations were referred to DOJ's Office of Professional Responsibility (OPR). The Task Force was headed by an Assistant Counsel from OPR and consisted of four career attorneys from DOJ's Criminal Division and a number of FBI inspectors and investigative agents. The Task Force submitted a 542 page report to OPR on June 10, 1994, which found numerous problems with the conduct of the FBI, the U.S. Marshals Service, and the U.S. Attorneys office in Idaho, and made recommendations for institutional changes to address the problems it found. It also concluded that portions of the rules of engagement issued by the FBI during the incident were unconstitutional under the circumstances, and that the second of two shots taken by a member of the FBI's Hostage Rescue Team (HRT), which resulted in the death of Vicki Weaver, was not reasonable. The Task Force recommended that the matter of the shooting be referred to a prosecutorial component of the Department for a determination as to whether a criminal investigation was appropriate. OPR reviewed the Task Force Report and transmitted the Report to the Deputy Attorney General with a memorandum that dissented from the recommendation that the shooting of Vicki Weaver by the HRT member be reviewed for prosecutorial merit based on the view that given the totality of circumstances, the agent's actions were not unreasonable. The Deputy Attorney referred the Task Force recommendation for prosecutorial review to the Criminal Section of the Civil Rights Division which concluded that there was no basis for criminal prosecution. The Task Force Report was the critical basis for the Subcommittee's inquiries during the hearings and its discussion and conclusions in its final report.[71]

Chapter 4

ASSESSMENT OF DOJ'S OPPOSITION TO CONGRESSIONAL ACCESS TO INFORMATION IN OPEN AND CLOSED LITIGATION FILES AND TO INTERNAL DELIBERATIVE MATERIALS

THE DEPARTMENT'S POSITION

The reasons advanced by the executive for declining to provide information to Congress about open and closed civil and criminal proceedings, most famously articulated by then Attorney General Robert Jackson in 1941, have included avoiding prejudicial pre-trial publicity, protecting the rights of innocent third parties, protecting the identity of confidential informants, preventing disclosure of the government's strategy in anticipated or pending judicial proceedings, avoiding the potentially chilling effect on the exercise of prosecutorial discretion by DOJ attorneys, and precluding interference with the President's constitutional duty to faithfully execute the laws all of which would "seriously prejudice law enforcement."[72]

Jackson's views were reiterated by Attorney General William French Smith in 1982 during the Superfund dispute, there applying the policy to documents "which are sensitive memoranda or notes by EPA attorneys and investigators reflecting enforcement strategy, legal analyses, lists of potential witnesses, settlement considerations and similar materials the disclosure of which might adversely affect a pending enforcement action, overall enforcement policy, or the rights of individuals. I continue to believe, as have my predecessors, that unrestricted dissemination of law enforcement files would prejudice the cause of effective law enforcement and, because the reasons for the policy of confidentiality are as sound and fundamental to the administration of justice today as they were forty years ago, I see no reason to depart from the consistent position of previous presidents and attorney generals." Acceding to congressional investigation demands, the Attorney General asserted, would make Congress "in a sense, a partner in the investigation" raising " a substantial danger that congressional pressures will influence the course of the investigation." This policy is said to be "premised in part on the fact that the Constitution vests in the President and his subordinates the responsibility to 'Take Care that the Laws be faithfully executed.'"[73]

Finally, in the 2001-2002 House Government Reform Committee investigation of the FBI misuse of informants, the Department maintained its historic position of withholding internal deliberative prosecutorial documents until just weeks before its eventual abandonment. In a February 1, 2002, letter to Chairman Burton, the DOJ Assistant Attorney General for Legislative Affairs explained;

> Our particular concern in the current controversy pertains to the narrow and especially sensitive categories of advice memoranda to the Attorney General and the deliberative documents making recommendations regarding whether or not to bring criminal charges against individuals. We believe that the public interest in avoiding the polarization of the criminal justice process required greater protection of those documents which, in turn, influences the accommodation process. This is not an "inflexible position," but rather a statement of a principled interest in ensuring the integrity of prosecutorial decision-making.[74]

Assessment of the Department's Position

1. Concerns with Pre-Trial Publicity, due Process, and Concurrent Investigations

As has been recounted previously, the Supreme Court has repeatedly reaffirmed the breadth of Congress' right to investigate the government's conduct of criminal and civil litigation.[75] The courts have also explicitly held that agencies may not deny Congress access to agency documents, even in situations where the inquiry may result in the exposure of criminal corruption or maladministration of agency officials. The Supreme Court has noted, "[B]ut surely a congressional committee which is engaged in a legitimate legislative investigation need not grind to a halt whenever responses to its inquiries might potentially be harmful to a witness in some distinct proceeding ... or when crime or wrongdoing is exposed."[76] The Court further explained:

> The suggestion made in dissent that the questions which petitioner refused to answer were 'outside the power of a committee to ask' under the Due Process Clause because they touched on matters then pending in judicial proceedings cannot be accepted for several reasons: First, the reasoning underlying this proposition is that these inquiries constituted a legislative encroachment on the judicial function. But such reasoning can hardly be limited to inquiries that may be germane to existing judicial proceedings: it would surely apply as well to inquiries calling for answers that my be used to the prejudice of witnesses in any future judicial proceeding. If such were the reach of 'due process' it would turn a witness' privilege against self-incrimination into a self-operating restraint on congressional inquiry, and would in effect *pro tanto* obliterate the need for that constitutional protection.[77]

Nor does the actual pendency of litigation disable Congress from the investigation of facts which have a bearing on that litigation, where the information sought is needed to determine what, if any, legislation should be enacted to prevent further ills.[78]

Although several lower court decisions have recognized that congressional hearings may have the result of generating prejudicial pre-trial publicity, they have not suggested that there are any constitutional or legal limitations on Congress' right to conduct an investigation during the pendency of judicial proceedings. Instead, the cases have suggested approaches, such as granting a continuance or a change of venue, to deal with the publicity problem.[79] For example, the court in one of the leading cases, *Delaney v. United States,* entertained "no doubt that the committee acted lawfully, within the constitutional powers of Congress duly delegated to it" but went on to describe the possible consequences of concurrent executive and congressional investigations:

> We think that the United States is put to a choice in this matter: If the United States, through its legislative department, acting conscientiously pursuant to its conception of the public interest, chooses to hold a public hearing inevitably resulting in such damaging publicity prejudicial to a

> person awaiting trial on a pending indictment, then the United States must accept the consequences that the judicial department, charged with the duty of assuring the defendant a fair trial before an impartial jury, may find it necessary to postpone the trial until by lapse of time the danger of the prejudice may reasonably be thought to have been substantially removed.[80]

The *Delaney* court distinguished the case of a congressional hearing generating publicity relating to an individual not under indictment at the time (as was Delaney):

> Such a situation may present important differences from the instant case. In such a situation the investigative function of Congress has its greatest utility: Congress is informing itself so that it may take appropriate legislative action; it is informing the Executive so that existing laws may be enforced; and it is informing the public so that democratic processes may be brought to bear to correct any disclosed executive laxity. Also, if as a result of such legislative hearing an indictment is eventually procured against the public official, then in the normal case there would be a much greater lapse of time between the publicity accompanying the public hearing and the trial of the subsequently indicted official than would be the case if the legislative hearing were held while the accused is awaiting trial on a pending indictment.[81]

The absence of indictment and the length of time between congressional hearing and criminal trial have been factors in courts rejecting claims that congressionally generated publicity prejudiced defendants.[82] Finally, in the context of adjudicatory administrative proceedings, courts on occasion have held that pressures emanating from questioning of agency decisionmakers by Members of Congress may be sufficient to undermine the impartiality of the proceeding.[83] But the courts have also made clear that mere inquiry and oversight of agency actions, including agency proceedings that are quasi-adjudicatory in nature, will not be held to rise to the level of political pressure designed to influence particular proceedings that would require judicial condemnation.[84]

Thus, the courts have recognized the potentially prejudicial effect congressional hearings can have on pending cases. While not questioning the prerogatives of Congress with respect to oversight and investigation, the cases pose a choice for the Congress: congressionally generated publicity may result in harming the prosecutorial effort of the Executive; but access to information under secure conditions can fulfill the congressional power of investigation and at the same time need not be inconsistent with the authority of the executive to pursue its case. Nonetheless, it remains a choice that is solely within Congress' discretion to make irrespective of the consequences. The observation of the Iran-Contra Independent Counsel is pertinent here: "The legislative branch has the power to decide whether it is more important perhaps to destroy a prosecution than to hold back testimony they need. They make that decision. It is not a judicial decision, or a legal decision, but a political decision of the highest importance."[85]

In the past the executive frequently has made a broader claim that prosecution is an inherently executive function and that congressional access to information related to the exercise of that function is thereby limited. Prosecutorial discretion is seen as off-limits to congressional inquiry and access demands are viewed as interfering with the discretion traditionally enjoyed by the prosecutor with respect to pursuing criminal cases.

2. Concerns over Revelations of Government Strategies or Methods or Weaknesses of Investigation

Attorney General and DOJ/OLC opinions raise concerns that congressional oversight that calls for information which reflects on the government's strategy or its methods or weaknesses is somehow inappropriate. Arguably, however, if this type of concern were recognized as enabling the blocking of congressional inquiry, it would end a major portion of legislative oversight. Congressional inquiries into foreign affairs and military matters call for information on strategy and weaknesses in national security matters; congressional probes into waste, fraud, and inefficiency in domestic operations calls for information on strategy and weaknesses. For Congress to forego such inquiries might signal an abandonment of its oversight duties: The best way to correct either bad law or bad administration is to closely examine these matters. The many examples congressional probes recounted above and in the Appendix to this report underline the efficacy and necessity of the revelation of such matters.

3. The Claim that Prosecution Is a Core Presidential Power Subject to Assertions of Executive Privilege

Initially, it must be noted that the Supreme Court has rejected the notion that prosecutorial discretion in criminal matters is an inherent or core executive function. Rather, the Court noted in *Morrison v. Olson,[86]* sustaining the validity of the appointment and removal conditions for independent counsels under the Ethics in Government Act, that the independent counsel's prosecutorial powers are executive in that they have "typically" been performed by Executive Branch officials, but held that the exercise of prosecutorial discretion is in no way "central" to the functioning of the Executive Branch.[87] The Court therefore rejected a claim that insulating the independent counsel from at-will presidential removal interfered with the President's duty to "take care" that the laws be faithfully executed. Interestingly, the *Morrison* Court took the occasion to reiterate the fundamental nature of Congress' oversight function (" ... receiving reports or other information and oversight of the independent counsel's activities ... [are] functions that we have recognized as generally incidental to the legislative function of Congress," citing *McGrain v. Daugherty*.)[88]

The breadth of *Morrison's* ruling that the prosecutorial function is not an exclusive function of the executive was made clear in a decision of the Ninth Circuit Court of Appeals in *United States ex rel Kelly* v. *The Boeing Co.*,[89] which upheld, against a broad based separation of powers attack, the constitutionality of the *qui tam* provisions of the False Claims Act vesting enforcement functions against agencies by private parties. Boeing argued, *inter alia*, that Congress could not vest enforcement functions outside the Executive Branch in private parties. Applying *Morrison* the appeals court emphatically rejected the contention.

> Before comparing the *qui tam* provisions of the FCA to the independent counsel provisions of the Ethics in Government Act, we must address Boeing's contention that only the Executive Branch has the power to enforce laws, and therefore to prosecute violations of law. *It is clear to us that no such absolute rule exists. Morrison* itself indicates otherwise because that decision validated the independent counsel provisions of the Ethics in Government Act even though it recognized that "it is undeniable that the Act reduces the amount of control or supervision that the Attorney General and, through him, the President exercises over the investigation and prosecution of a certain class of alleged criminal activity." 487 U.S. at 695. The Court also stated in *Morrison* that "there is no real dispute that the functions performed by the independent counsel are `executive' in the sense that they are law enforcement functions that typically have been undertaken by officials within the Executive Branch." 487 U.S. at 692 (emphasis added). Use of the world "typically" in that sentence, considered in light of the Court's ultimate conclusion upholding the independent counsel provisions, must mean that prosecutorial functions need not always be undertaken by Executive Branch officials. See Stephanie A.J. Dangel, Note, Is Prosecution a Core Executive Function? Morrison v. Olson and the

> Framers' Intent, 99 Yale L.J. 1069, 1070 (1990)(Framers intended that prosecution would be undertaken by but not constitutionally assigned to executive officials, and that such officials would typically but not always prosecute). *Thus, we reject Boeing's assertion that all prosecutorial power of any kind belongs to the Executive Branch.[90]*

Prosecution, not being a core or exclusive function of the Executive, cannot claim the constitutional stature of Congress' oversight prerogative. In the absence of a credible claim of encroachment or aggrandizement by the legislature of essential Executive powers, the Supreme Court has held the appropriate judicial test is one that determines whether the challenged legislative action "`prevents the Executive Branch from accomplishing its assigned functions'," and, if so, "`whether that impact is justified by an overriding need to promote objectives within the constitutional authority of Congress'."[91]

Congressional oversight and access to documents and testimony, unlike the action of a court, cannot stop a prosecution or set limits on the management of a particular case. Access to information by itself would not seem to disturb the authority and discretion of the Executive Branch to decide whether to prosecute a case. The assertion of prosecutorial discretion in the face of a congressional demand for information is arguably akin to the "generalized" claim of confidentiality made in the Watergate executive privilege cases. That general claim — lacking in specific demonstration of disruption of executive functions — was held to be overcome by the more focused demonstration of need for information by a coordinate branch of government.[92]

Given the legitimacy of congressional oversight and investigation of the law enforcement agencies of government, and the need for access to information pursuant to such activities, a claim of prosecutorial discretion by itself would not seem to be sufficient to defeat a congressional need for information. The congressional action itself does not and cannot dictate prosecutorial policy or decisions in particular cases. Congress may enact statutes that influence prosecutorial policy, and information relating to enforcement of the laws would seem necessary to perform that legislative function. Thus, under the standard enunciated in *Morrison v. Olson* and *Nixon v. Administrator of General Services,* the fact that information is sought on the executive's enforcement of criminal laws would not in itself seem to preclude congressional inquiry.

In light of the Supreme Court's consistent support of the power of legislative inquiry, and in the absence of a countervailing constitutional prerogative of the executive, reviewing courts may be disposed to be "sensitive to the legislative importance of congressional committees on oversight and investigations and recognize that their interest in the objective and efficient operation of ... agencies serves a legitimate and wholesome function with which we should not lightly interfere."[93] More particularly, future judicial decisions involving presidential claims of privilege with respect to prosecutorial decisionmaking by DOJ likely will be informed by two District of Columbia Circuit rulings that filled important gaps in the law of presidential privilege that had been developed between 1977 and 1983.[94]

The *Nixon* and post-Watergate cases established the broad contours of the presidential communications privilege. Under those precedents, the privilege, which is constitutionally rooted, could be invoked by the President when asked to produce documents or other materials or information that reflect presidential decisionmaking and deliberations that he believes should remain confidential. If the President does so, the materials become presumptively privileged. The privilege, however, is qualified, not absolute, and can be overcome by an adequate showing of need. Finally, while reviewing courts have expressed reluctance to balance executive privilege claims against a congressional demand for information, they have acknowledged they will do so if the political branches have tried in good faith but failed to reach an accommodation.

However, until the District of Columbia Circuit's 1997 ruling in *In re Sealed Case,[95]* and its 2004 ruling in *Judicial Watch, Inc. v. Department of Justice*,[96] these judicial decisions had left important gaps in the law of presidential privilege which increasingly became focal points, if not the source, of interbranch confrontations. Among the more significant issues left open included whether the President has to have actually seen or been familiar with the disputed matter; whether the presidential privilege encompasses documents and information developed by, or in the possession of, officers and employees in the departments and agencies of the Executive Branch; whether the privilege encompasses all communications with respect to which the President may be interested or is it confined to presidential decisionmaking and, if so, is it limited to any particular type of presidential decisionmaking; and precisely what kind of demonstration of need must be shown to justify release of materials that qualify for the privilege. The unanimous panel in *In re Sealed Case* addressed each of these issues in a manner that may have drastically altered the future legal playing field in resolving such disputes. The recent ruling in the *Judicial Watch* case reinforces that likelihood.[97]

In re Sealed Case (Espy)[98] arose out of an Office of Independent Counsel (OIC) investigation of former Agriculture Secretary Mike Espy. When allegations of improprieties by Espy surfaced in March of 1994, President Clinton ordered the White House Counsel's Office to investigate and report to him so he could determine what action, if any, he should undertake. The White House Counsel's Office prepared a report for the President, which was publically released on October 11, 1994. The President never saw any of the underlying or supporting documents to the report. Espy had announced his resignation on October 3, to be effective on December 31. Meanwhile, the Independent Counsel had been appointed on September 9 and the grand jury issued a subpoena for all documents that were accumulated or used in preparation of the report on October 14, three days after the report's issuance. The President withheld 84 documents, claiming both the executive and deliberative process privileges for all documents. A motion to compel was resisted on the basis of the claimed privileges and after *in camera* review the district court quashed the subpoena, but in its written opinion did not discuss the documents in any detail and provided no analysis of the grand jury's need for the documents. The appeals court reversed.

At the outset, the court's opinion carefully distinguishes between the "presidential communications privilege" and the "deliberative process privilege." Both, the court observed, are executive privileges designed to protect the confidentiality of executive branch decisionmaking. The deliberative process privilege applies to executive branch officials generally, is a common law privilege which requires a lower threshold of need to be overcome, and "disappears altogether when there is any reason to believe government misconduct has occurred."[99]

On the other hand, the court explained, the presidential communications privilege is rooted in "constitutional separation of powers principles and the President's unique constitutional role" and applies only to "direct decisionmaking by the President."[100] The privilege may be overcome only by a substantial showing that "the subpoenaed materials likely contain[] important evidence" and that "the evidence is not available with due diligence elsewhere."[101] The presidential privilege applies to all documents in their entirety[102] and covers final and post-decisional materials as well as pre-deliberative ones.[103]

Turning to the chain of command issue, the court held that the presidential communications privilege must cover communications made or received by presidential advisers in the course of preparing advice for the President even if those communications are not made directly to the

President. The court rested its conclusion on "the President's dependence on presidential advisers and the inability of the deliberative process privilege to provide advisers with adequate freedom from the public spotlight" and "the need to provide sufficient elbow room for advisers to obtain information from all knowledgeable sources".[104] Thus the privilege will "apply both to communications which these advisers solicited and received from others as well as those they authored themselves. The privilege must also extend to communications authored or received in response to a solicitation by members of a presidential adviser's staff."[105]

The court, however, was acutely aware of the dangers to open government that a limitless extension of the privilege risks and carefully cabined its reach by explicitly confining it to White House staff, and not staff in the agencies, and then only to White House staff that has "operational proximity" to direct presidential decisionmaking.

> We are aware that such an extension, unless carefully circumscribed to accomplish the purposes of the privilege, could pose a significant risk of expanding to a large swath of the executive branch a privilege that is bottomed on a recognition of the unique role of the President. In order to limit this risk, the presidential communications privilege should be construed as narrowly as is consistent with ensuring that the confidentiality of the President's decisionmaking process is adequately protected. Not every person who plays a role in the development of presidential advice, no matter how remote and removed from the President, can qualify for the privilege. In particular, the privilege should not extend to staff outside the White House in executive branch agencies. Instead, the privilege should apply only to communications authored or solicited and received by those members of an immediate White House advisor's staff who have broad and significant responsibility for investigation and formulating the advice to be given the President on the particular matter to which the communications relate. Only communications at that level are close enough to the President to be revelatory of his deliberations or to pose a risk to the candor of his advisers. *See* AAPS, 997 F.2d at 910 (it is "operational proximity" to the President that matters in determining whether "[t]he President's confidentiality interests" is implicated)(emphasis omitted).
>
> Of course, the privilege only applies to communications that these advisers and their staff author or solicit and receive in the course of performing their function of advising the President on official government matters. This restriction is particularly important in regard to those officials who exercise substantial independent authority or perform other functions in addition to advising the President, and thus are subject to FOIA and other open government statutes. See

> *Armstrong v. Executive Office of the President,* 90 F.3d 553, 558 (D.C. Cir. 1996), *cert denied* — U.S. — -, 1 17 S.Ct. 1842, 137 L. Ed.2d 1046 (1997). The presidential communications privilege should never serve as a means of shielding information regarding governmental operations that do not call ultimately for direct decisionmaking by the President. If the government seeks to assert the presidential communications privilege in regard to particular communications of these "dual hat" presidential advisers, the government bears the burden of proving that the communications occurred in conjunction with the process of advising the President.[106]

The appeals court's limitation of the presidential communications privilege to "direct decisionmaking by the President" makes it imperative to identify the type of decisionmaking to which it refers. A close reading of the opinion makes it arguable that it is meant to encompass only those functions that form the core of presidential authority, involving what the court characterized as "quintessential and non-delegable Presidential power."[107] In the case before it the court was specifically referring to the President's Article II appointment and removal power which was the focal point of the advice he sought in the Espy matter. But it is clear from the context of the opinion that the description was meant to juxtapose appointment and removal power in contrast with "presidential powers and responsibilities" that "can be exercised or performed without the President's direct involvement, pursuant to a presidential delegation of authority or statutory framework."[108] The reference the court uses to illustrate the latter category is the President's Article II duty "to take care that the laws are faithfully executed," a constitutional direction that the courts have consistently held not to be a source of presidential power but rather an obligation on the President to see to it that the will of Congress is carried out by the executive bureaucracy.[109]

The appeals court, then, would appear to be confining the parameters of the newly formulated presidential communications privilege by tying it to those Article II functions that are identifiable as "quintessential and non-delegable," which would appear to include, in addition to the appointment and removal powers, the commander-in-chief power, the sole authority to receive ambassadors and other public ministers, the power to negotiate treaties, and the power to grant pardons and reprieves. On the other hand, decisionmaking vested by law in agency heads such as prosecutorial decisionmaking, rulemaking, environmental policy, consumer protection, workplace safety and labor relations, among others, would not necessarily be covered. Of course, the President's role in supervising and coordinating (but not displacing) decisionmaking in the executive branch remains unimpeded.

But his communications would presumably not be cloaked by constitutional privilege.

Such a reading of this critical passage is consonant with the court's view of the source and purpose of the presidential communications privilege and its expressed need to confine it as narrowly as possible. Relying on *United States* v. *Nixon ,[110]* the In *re Sealed Case* court identifies "the President's Article II powers and responsibilities as the constitutional basis of the presidential communications privilege. Since the Constitution assigns these responsibilities to the President alone, arguably the privilege of confidentiality that derives from it also should be the President's alone."[111] Again relying on *Nixon* the appeals court pinpoints the essential purpose of the privilege: "[Tlhe privilege is rooted in the need for confidentiality to ensure that presidential decisionmaking is of the highest caliber, informed by honest advice and knowledge. Confidentiality is what ensures the expression of 'candid, objective, and even blunt or harsh opinions' and the comprehensive exploration of all policy alternatives before a presidential course of action is selected."[112] The limiting safeguard is that the privilege will apply in those instances where the Constitution provides that the President alone must make a decision. "The presidential communications privilege should never serve as a means of shielding information regarding governmental operations that do not call ultimately for direct decisionmaking by the President."[113]

The District of Columbia Circuit's 2004 decision in *Judicial Watch, Inc. v. Department of Justice[114]* appears to lend substantial support to the above-expressed understanding of *Espy. Judicial Watch* involved requests for documents concerning pardon applications and pardon grants reviewed by the Justice Department's Office of the Pardon Attorney and the Deputy Attorney General for consideration by President Clinton.[115] Some 4,300 documents were withheld on the grounds that they were protected by the presidential communications and deliberative process privileges. The district court held that because the materials sought had been produced for the sole purpose of advising the President on a "quintessential and non-delegable Presidential power" — the exercise of the President's constitutional pardon authority — the extension of the presidential communications privilege to internal Justice Department documents which had not been "solicited and received" by the President or the Office of the President was warranted.[116] The appeals court reversed, concluding that "internal agency documents that are not solicited and received by the President or his Office are instead protected against disclosure, if at all, by the deliberative process privilege."[117]

Guided by the analysis of the *Espy* ruling, the panel majority emphasized that the "solicited and received" limitation "is necessitated by the principles underlying the presidential communications privilege, and a recognition of the dangers of expanding it too far."[118] *Espy* teaches, the appeals court explained, that the privilege may be invoked only when presidential advisers in close proximity to the President who have significant responsibility for advising him on non-delegable matters requiring direct presidential decisionmaking, have solicited and received such documents or communications or the President has received them himself. In rejecting the Government's argument that the privilege should be applicable to all departmental and agency communications related to the Deputy Attorney General's pardon recommendations for the President, the panel majority held that "such a bright-line rule is inconsistent with the nature and principles of the presidential communications privilege, as well as the goal of serving the public interest. Communications never received by the President or his Office are unlikely to be revelatory of his deliberations ... nor is there any reason to fear that the Deputy Attorney General's candor or the quality of the Deputy's pardon recommendations would be sacrificed if the presidential communications privilege did not apply to internal documents. Any pardon documents, reports or recommendations that the Deputy Attorney General submits to the Office of the President, and any direct communications the Deputy or the Pardon Attorney may have with the White House Counsel or other immediate Presidential advisors will remain protected. It is only those documents and recommendations of Department staff that are not submitted by the Deputy Attorney General for the President and are not otherwise received by the Office of the President, that do not fall under the presidential communications privilege"[119] Indeed, the *Judicial Watch* panel makes it clear that the *Espy* rationale would preclude cabinet department heads from being treated as being part of the President's immediate personal staff or as some unit of the Office of the President:

> Extension of the presidential communications privilege to the Attorney General's delegatee, the Deputy Attorney General, and his staff, on down to the Pardon Attorney and his staff, with the attendant implication for expansion to other Cabinet officers and their staffs, would, as the court pointed out in In re Sealed Case, pose a significant risk of expanding to a large swatch of the executive branch a privilege that is bottomed on a recognition of the unique role of the President.[120]

The *Judicial Watch* majority took great pains to explain why *Espy* and the case before it differed from the *Nixon* and post-Watergate cases: "Until

In re Sealed Case, the privilege had been tied specifically to direct communications of the President with his immediate White House advisors"[121] The *Espy* court, it explained, was for the first time confronted with the question whether communications that the President's closest advisors make in the course of preparing advise for the President which the President never saw should also be covered by the presidential privilege. The *Espy* court's answer was to "espouse[ ] a 'limited extension' of the privilege' 'down the chain of command' beyond the President to his immediate White House advisors only," recognizing "the need to ensure that the President would receive full and frank advice with regard to his non-delegable appointment and removal powers, but was also wary of undermining countervailing considerations such as openness in government.... Hence, the [*Espy*] court determined that while 'communications authored or solicited and received' by immediate White House advisors in the Office of the President could qualify under the privilege, communications of staff outside the White House in executive branch agencies that were not solicited and received by such White House advisors could not."[122]

The situation before the *Judicial Watch* court tested the *Espy* principles. While the presidential decision involved — exercise of the President's pardon power — was certainly a non-delegable, core presidential function, the operating officials involved, the Deputy Attorney General and the Pardon Attorney, were deemed to be too remote from the President and his senior White House advisors to be protected. The court conceded that functionally those officials were performing a task directly related to the pardon decision but concluded that an organizational test was more appropriate for confining the potentially broad sweep that would result from a functional test; under the latter test, there would be no limit to the coverage of the presidential communications privilege. In such circumstances, the panel majority concluded, the lesser protections of the deliberative process privilege would have to suffice.[123]

4. The Claim of Deliberative Process Privilege

Espy and *Judicial Watch,* taken together with *Morrison* v. *Olson's* holding that prosecution is not a core or exclusive function of the executive, and *McGrain* v. *Daugherty's* understanding that Congress' access to prosecutorial information is founded on its plenary authority to create, empower and fund the activities of the Department, raise serious doubts as to the propriety of the claim to a presidential communications privilege in a situation involving internal agency deliberative information. Rather, a withholding claim based on "deliberative process" arguably must be tested as one of the common law privileges available to executive agencies that may be overcome by a showing of need by an investigatory body and, as *Espy* noted, "disappears" upon a reasonable belief by such investigating body that government misconduct has occurred. Thus, a demonstration of need by a jurisdictional committee in most circumstances would appear to be sufficient, and a plausible showing of fraud, waste, abuse or maladministration would likely be conclusive.

Even before *Espy,* courts and committees had consistently resisted withholding claims of agencies as attempts to establish a species of agency privilege designed to thwart congressional oversight efforts. Thus it has been pointed out that the claim that internal communications need to be "frank" and "open" does not merit special support and that coupling that characterization with the notion that those communications were part of a "deliberative process" will not add any weight to the argument. In effect, such arguments have been seen as attempting to justify a withholding from Congress on the same grounds that an agency would use to withhold such documents from a citizen requester under Exemption 5 of the Freedom of Information Act (FOIA).[124]

Such a line of argument is likely to be found to be without substantial basis. As has been indicated above, Congress has vastly greater powers of investigation than those of citizen FOIA requesters. Moreover, in the FOIA itself, Congress carefully provided that the exemption section "is not authority to withhold information from Congress."[125] The D.C. Circuit, in *Murphy v. Department of the Army*,[126] explained that FOIA exemptions were no basis for withholding from Congress because of:

> the obvious purpose of the Congress to carve out for itself a special right of access to privileged information not shared by others ... . Congress, whether as a body, through committees, or otherwise, must have the widest possible access to executive branch information if it is to perform its manifold responsibilities effectively. If one consequence of the facilitation of such access is that some information will be disclosed to congressional authorities but not to private persons, that is but an incidental consequence of the need for informed and effective lawmakers.[127]

Further, it may be contended that the ability of an agency to assert the need for candor to ensure the efficacy of internal deliberations as a means of avoiding congressional information demands would severely undermine the oversight process. If that were sufficient, an agency would be encouraged to disclose only that which supports its positions, and withhold that with flaws, limitations, unwanted implications, or other embarrassments. Oversight would cease to become an investigative exercise of gathering the whole evidence, and become little more than a set-piece in which an agency decides what to present in a controlled "show and tell" performance.

Moreover, every federal official, including attorneys, could assert the imperative of timidity — that congressional oversight, by holding up to scrutiny the advice he gives, will frighten him away from giving frank opinions, or discourage others from asking him for them. This argument, not surprisingly, has failed over the years to persuade legislative bodies to cease oversight. Indeed, when the Supreme Court discussed the "secret law" doctrine in *NLRB v. Sears, Roebuck and Co.[128]* it addressed why federal officials — including those giving legal opinions — need not hide behind such fears:

> The probability that an agency employee will be inhibited from freely advising a decisionmaker for fear that his advice, if *adopted*, will become public is slight. First, when adopted, the reasoning becomes that of agency and becomes its responsibility to defend. Second, agency employees will generally be encouraged rather than discouraged by public knowledge that their policy suggestions have been adopted by the agency. Moreover, the public interest in knowing the reasons for a policy actually adopted by an agency supports ...[disclosure].[129]

Arguably, a "chilling effect" argument needs to be demonstrated concretely in particular cases or else it would overwhelm investigative prerogatives.

Chapter 5

Concluding Observations

Congress has an established right and judicially recognized prerogative, pursuant to its constitutional authority to legislate, to receive from officers and employees of the agencies and departments of the United States accurate and truthful information regarding the federal programs and policies administered by such employees and agencies. As stated by the Supreme Court, "[a] legislative body cannot legislate wisely or effectively in the absence of information regarding conditions which the legislation is intended to affect or change"[130], and thus, what observers might characterize as political gamesmanship must yield, according to the courts, to the clear public interest of providing the peoples' elected representatives in the Congress with accurate and truthful information upon which to effectively fashion or revise the laws for the Nation. There is no countervailing right or interest for a federal official in an agency or department to intentionally withhold, conceal or prevent the disclosure of truthful public policy information from the United States Congress concerning legislation affecting the programs and policies administered by that agency, when requested by a jurisdictional committee of the Congress. This understanding applies with equal force to the law enforcement activities of the Department of Justice. As detailed in this report, as a matter of law, buttressed by 85 years history and practice, congressional committees with jurisdiction and authority that have exercised the full panoply of oversight and investigatory power available to them, have consistently gained access to needed information from the Department in the form of documents or testimony from any component of the agency, regardless of the subject matter involved and irrespective of the grade level of the officer or employee with the information or required knowledge.

Judicial rulings over the past two decades rejecting assorted presidential prerogatives that might deny congressional access to agency information appear to have buttressed congressional oversight authority. The Supreme Court's ruling in *Morrison* v. *Olsen* casts significant doubt whether prosecutorial discretion is a core presidential power over which executive privilege may be asserted, a doubt that has been magnified by the appellate court rulings in *Espy* and *Judicial Watch*. In those latter decisions, assertion of the presidential communications privilege was held to be limited to "quintessential and nondelegable presidential power" and is confined to communications to advisors in "operational proximity" with the President. Those decisions indicate that core powers include only decisions that the President alone can make under the Constitution: appointment and removal, pardoning, receiving ambassadors and other public ministers, negotiating treaties, and exercising powers as Commander-in-Chief. *Espy* strongly hinted, and *Judicial Watch* made clear, that the protection of the presidential communications privilege extends only to the boundaries of the White House and the Executive office complex and not to the departments and agencies, even if the actions there related to a core power, unless they are "solicited and received" by a close White House advisor or the President himself. *Judicial Watch*, which dealt with pardon documents in DOJ that had not been "solicited and received" by a close White House advisor, determined that "the need for the presidential communications privilege becomes more attenuated the further away the advisors are from the President [which] affects the extent to which the contents of the President's communications can be inferred from predecisional communications."[131] Of course these rulings did not involve congressional requests, but until reviewed by the Supreme Court they are the law of the circuit most likely to hear and rule on future claims of presidential privilege.

This is not meant to gainsay or dismiss out of hand the weight and applicability of the DOJ policy arguments in particular situations and circumstances. Our review of the historical record of congressional inquiries and experiences with committee investigations of DOJ has indicated that committees normally have been restrained by prudential considerations informed by weighing the considerations of legislative need, public policy, and the statutory duty of congressional committees to engage in continuous oversight against the potential burdens and harms that may be imposed on DOJ or any other agency if deliberative process matter is publically disclosed. The sensitive law enforcement concerns and duties of the Justice Department often have been seen to merit that substantial weight be given the agency's deliberative processes in the absence of a reasonable belief of a jurisdictional committee that government misconduct has occurred. Rather we have addressed here the oft-repeated rhetorical notion that the Department never has allowed congressional access to open or closed litigation files or other "sensitive" internal deliberative process matter and examine the legal weight to assertions to withhold vis a vis congressional oversight authority.

APPENDIX. SELECTED CONGRESSIONAL INVESTIGATIONS OF THE DEPARTMENT OF JUSTICE, 1920-2007

This appendix consists of brief summaries of 18 significant congressional investigations of the Department of Justice which involved either open or closed investigations in which the Department agreed to supply documents pertaining to those investigations, including prosecutorial decisionmaking memoranda and correspondence, and to provide high ranking officials as well as subordinate employees such as line attorneys and investigative personnel for staff interviews and for testimony before committees.

PALMER RAIDS

In 1920 and 1921, investigations were held in the Senate and House into the so-called "Palmer raids" in which, under the direction of Attorney General A. Mitchell Palmer, thousands of suspected Communists and others allegedly advocating the overthrow of the government were arrested and deported. See Charges of Illegal Practices of the Department of Justice: Hearings Before a Subcommittee of the Senate Committee on the Judiciary, 66th Congress, 3d Session (1921)(hereinafter "Senate Palmer Hearings"); Attorney General A. Mitchell Palmer on Charges Made Against Department of Justice by Louis F . Post and Others: Hearings Before the House Committee on Rules, 66th Congress, 2d Session (1920)(hereinafter "House Palmer Hearings"). Attorney General Palmer, accompanied by his Special

Assistant, J. Edgar Hoover, during three days of testimony at the Senate hearings discussed the details of numerous deportation cases, including cases which were on appeal. Senate Palmer Hearings at 38-98, 421-86, 539-63. House Palmer Hearings at 3-209. In support of his testimony, Palmer provided the Subcommittee with various Department memoranda and correspondence, including Bureau of Investigation reports concerning the deportation cases. E.g., Senate Palmer Hearings at 431-43, 458- 69, 472-76. Among the materials provided were the Department's confidential instructions to the Bureau outlining the procedures to be followed in the surveillance and arrest of the suspected Communists, *id.* at 12-14, 18-19, and a lengthy "memorandum of comments and analysis" prepared by one of Palmer's special assistants, which responded to a District Court opinion, at the time under appeal, critical of the Department's actions in these deportation cases, *id.* at 484-538. See also, Harlan Grant Cohen, "The (Un)Favorable Judgment of History: Deportation Hearings, the Palmer Raids, and the Meaning of History," 78 NYU. L. Rev. 1431, 1451-1456 (2003)(recounting historical context of Palmer Raids).

Teapot Dome

Several years later, the Senate conducted an investigation of the Teapot Dome scandal. While the Senate Committee on Public Lands and Surveys focused on the actions of the Department of the Interior in leasing naval oil reserves, a Senate select committee was constituted to investigate "charges of misfeasance and nonfeasance in the Department of Justice," *McGrain v. Daugherty,* 273 U.S. 135, 151 (1927), in failing to prosecute the malefactors in the Department of the Interior, as well as other cases. Investigation of Hon. Harry M. Daugherty, Formerly Attorney General of the United States: Hearings Before the Senate Select Committee on Investigation of the Attorney General, vols. 1-3, 68th Congress, 1st Session (1924). The select committee heard from scores of present and former attorneys and agents of the Department and its Bureau of Investigation, who offered detailed testimony about specific instances of the Department's failure to prosecute alleged meritorious cases. Not all of the cases upon which testimony was offered were closed, as one of the committee's goals in its questioning was to identify cases in which the statute of limitations had not run out and prosecution was still possible. *See, e.g., id.* at 1495-1503, 1529-30, 2295-96.

The committee also obtained access to Department documentation, including prosecutorial memoranda, on a wide range of matters. However, given the charges of widespread corruption in the Department and the imminent resignation of Attorney General Daugherty, it would appear that some of the documents furnished the committee early in the hearings may have been volunteered by the witnesses and not officially provided by the Department. Although Attorney General Daugherty had promised cooperation with the committee, and had agreed to provide access to at least the files of closed cases, *id.* at 1120, such cooperation apparently had not been forthcoming, *id.* at 1078- 79.

In two instances immediately following Daugherty's resignation, the committee was refused access to confidential Bureau of Investigation investigative reports pending the appointment of a new Attorney General who could advise the President about such production, *id.* at 1015-16 and 1159-60, though witnesses from the Department were permitted to testify about the investigations that were the subject of the investigative reports and even to read at the hearings from the investigative reports. With the appointment of the new Attorney General, Harlan F. Stone, the committee was granted broad access to Department files. Committee Chairman Smith Brookhard remarked that "[Stone] is furnishing us with all the files we want, whereas the former Attorney General, Mr. Daugherty, refused nearly all that we asked." *Id.* at 2389. For example, with the authorization of the new Attorney General, an accountant with the Department who had led an investigation of fraudulent sales of property by the Alien Property Custodian's office appeared and produced his confidential reports to the Bureau of Investigation. The reports described the factual findings from his investigation and his recommendations for further action, and included the names of companies and individuals suspected of making false claims. The Department had not acted on those recommendations, though the cases had not been closed. *Id.* at 1495-1547. A similar investigative report, concerning an inquiry into the disappearance of large quantities of liquor under the control of the Department during the prior administration of President Harding, was also produced. *Id.* at 1790.

As part of its investigation, the select committee issued a subpoena for the testimony of Mally S. Daugherty, the brother of the Attorney General. After Mally Daugherty failed to respond to the subpoena, the Senate sent its Deputy Sergeant at Arms to take him into custody and bring him before the Senate. Daugherty petitioned in federal court for a writ of *habeas corpus* arguing that the Senate in its investigation had exceeded its constitutional powers. The case ultimately reached the Supreme Court, where, in a landmark decision, *McGrain v. Daugherty,* 273 U.S. 135 (1927), the Court upheld the Senate's authority to investigate these charges concerning the Department:

> [T]he subject to be investigated was the administration of the Department of Justice — whether its functions were being properly discharged or were being neglected or misdirected, and particularly whether the Attorney General and his assistants were performing or neglecting their duties in respect of the institution and prosecution of proceedings to punish crimes and enforce appropriate remedies against the wrongdoers — specific instances of alleged neglect being recited. Plainly the subject was one on which legislation could be had and would be materially aided by the information which the investigation was calculated to elicit.
> 273 U.S. at 177.

In another Teapot Dome case that reached the Supreme Court, *Sinclair v. United States,* 279 U.S. 263 (1929), a different witness at the Congressional hearings refused to provide answers, and was prosecuted for contempt of Congress. The witness had noted that a lawsuit had been commenced between the government and the Mammoth Oil Company, and declared, "I shall reserve any evidence I may be able to give for those courts... and shall respectfully decline to answer any questions propounded by your committee." *Id.* at 290. The Supreme Court upheld the witness' conviction for contempt of Congress. The Court considered and rejected in unequivocal terms the witness's contention that the pendency of lawsuits provided an excuse for withholding information. Neither the laws directing that such lawsuits be instituted, nor the lawsuits themselves, "operated to divest the Senate, or the committee, of power further to investigate the actual administration of the land laws." *Id.* at 295.

The Court further explained: "It may be conceded that Congress is without authority to compel disclosure for the purpose of aiding the prosecution of pending suits; but the authority of that body, directly or through its committees to require pertinent disclosures in aid of its own constitutional power is not abridged because the information sought to be elicited may also be of use in such suits." *Id.* at 295.

Investigations of DOJ During the 1950's

In 1952, a special House subcommittee was constituted to conduct an inquiry into the administration of the Department of Justice. The subcommittee conducted a lengthy investigation from 1952 to 1953, developing thousands of pages of testimony on a range of allegations of abuses and inefficiencies in the Department. Investigations of the Department of Justice: Hearings Before the Special Subcommittee to Investigate the Department of Justice of the House Committee on the Judiciary, parts 1 and 2, 82d Congress, 2d Session (1952), parts 1 and 2, 83d Congress, lst Session (l953)(hereafter "DOJ Investigation Hearings"). The subcommittee summarized its conclusions about its inquiries during the 82d Congress in Investigation of the Department of Justice, H.R. Rep. No.1079, 83d Congress, 1st Session (1953)(hereinafter "DOJ Investigation Report"). Among the subjects of inquiry considered during these hearings were the following:

1. Grand Jury Curbing

Extensive testimony was heard about a charge that the Department had attempted improperly to curb a grand jury inquiry in St. Louis into the failure to enforce federal tax fraud laws. After taking testimony in executive session from one witness, the subcommittee suspended its hearings on this subject pending the discharge of the grand jury. DOJ Investigation Hearings at 753. The subcommittee resumed its hearings several months later, at which time testimony was taken from the former Attorney General, a former Assistant Attorney General, the Chief of the appellate section of the Tax Division, and an Assistant U .S. Attorney. Several members of the St. Louis grand jury also testified before the subcommittee. In addition to intradepartmental correspondence, *see id.* at 1256-57, 1270- 71, among the materials that the subcommittee reviewed and included in the public record were transcripts of telephone conversations between various Department attorneys concerning the grand jury investigation. *Id.* at 759-66.[132]

The subcommittee began its hearings on the handling of the St. Louis grand jury with a statement emphasizing that its interest "is merely to ascertain whether or not there was in fact any attempt by the Department of Justice to influence the grand jury in its investigation," *id.* at 754, and that "the members of the subcommittee and counsel are aware of the rule of strict secrecy surrounding the proceedings of any grand jury . Mindful of that, our questioning will not touch upon any specific case or evidence that may have been presented to the grand jury." *Id.* The subcommittee's questions to the grand jurors focused on efforts by Department attorneys to prevent them from conducting a thorough investigation and on whether the grand jury had been pressured by those attorneys to issue a report absolving the government of impropriety in its handling of tax fraud cases. *Id.* at 766-808. Similar questions were asked of the present and former Department attorneys who testified, *id.* at 808-894, 1064-1117, 1256-1318, and at one point the subcommittee asked for, and an Assistant U .S. Attorney provided, the names of certain witnesses who had appeared before the grand jury. *Id.* at 811. Later that same year, the subcommittee examined similar charges of interference by the Department with another grand jury, which had been investigating Communist infiltration of the United Nations. The subcommittee received testimony from a number of grand jurors and Department attorneys, including then Criminal Division attorney Roy Cohn. *Id.* at 1653-1812. The subcommittee's chief counsel again cautioned that "[t]he sanctity of the grand jury as a process of American justice must be protected at all costs," and stated that the subcommittee was seeking information solely relating to attempts to delay or otherwise influence the grand jurors' deliberations, not which would reveal the actual testimony of witnesses appearing before them. *Id.* at 1579-80.

2. Prosecution of Routine Cases

Attorney General McGrath resigned in April 1952, in part in response to the evidence uncovered by the subcommittee of corruption in the Department, particularly in the Tax Division. As a result of the replacement of McGrath by James P. McGranery, and the Administration's concern about these reports of corruption, the subcommittee observed "a new and refreshing attitude of cooperation which soon appeared at all levels in the Department of Justice." DOJ Investigation Report at 69. The subcommittee declared that "its work has been limited only by the capacity of its staff to digest the sheer volume of available fact and documentary evidence relating to the Department's work. Everything that has been requested has been furnished, including file materials and administrative memoranda which had previously been withheld." *Id.*

For example, in investigating charges that the Department was often dilatory in its handling of routine cases, the subcommittee staff undertook a detailed analysis of a number of cases in which delay was alleged to have occurred. To demonstrate publicly the nature of this problem, the subcommittee chose a procurement fraud case that had been recently closed, and conducted a "public file review" of the case at a subcommittee hearing. Attorneys from the Department at the hearing went document by document through the Department's file in the case. DOJ Investigative Hearings (82d

Congress) at 895-964. The subcommittee was granted access to all of the documentation collected in the case, with the exception of confidential FBI reports which the subcommittee had agreed not to seek. However, certain communications from the FBI to the Department concerning the prosecution of the case were provided. *Id.* at 897.

3. New York City Police Brutality

During the 83d Congress, the subcommittee turned to allegations that the Criminal Division had entered into an agreement with the New York City Police Department not to prosecute instances of police brutality by New York police officers that might be violations of federal civil rights statutes. The subcommittee stated that its purpose was not to inquire into the merits of particular cases, only to ascertain whether such an arrangement had been entered into between the Justice Department and the New York City police. DOJ Investigation Hearings (83d Congress) at 26. Justice Department witnesses had also been instructed by the Attorney General not to discuss the merits of any pending cases. *Id.*

Department witnesses included a former Attorney General, several present and former Assistant Attorneys General, as well as other Department attorneys and FBI agents *Id.* at 25-294. The substance of earlier meetings between Department officials and the New York City Police Commissioner in which this arrangement was allegedly agreed to was probed in depth. Although questions concerning the merits of specific cases were avoided, the subcommittee obtained from these witnesses a chronology of the Department's actions in a number of cases. The subcommittee received Department memoranda and correspondence, as well as telephone transcripts of the intradepartmental conversations of a United States Attorney. *Id.* at 62-63, 233-34, 239-41, 258-59, 262, 269-73.

INVESTIGATION OF CONSENT DECREE PROGRAM

In 1957 and 1958, the Antitrust Subcommittee of the House Judiciary Committee conducted an inquiry into the negotiation and enforcement of consent decrees by the Antitrust Division, and their competitive effect, with particular emphasis on consent decrees that had been recently entered into with the oil-pipeline industry and AT and T. See Consent Degree Program of the Department of Justice: Hearings before the Antitrust Subcomm.

(Subcomm. No.5) of the House Comm. on the Judiciary, parts I and II, 85th Cong., 1st and 2d Sess. (1957-58)(hereafter "Consent Decree Hearings"); Antitrust Subcomm. (Subcomm. No.5), 86th Cong., 1st Sess., Report on Consent Decree Program of the Department of Justice (Comm. Print 1959)(hereafter "Consent Decree Report"). The subcommittee developed a 4,492-page hearing record, holding seventeen days of hearings on the AT and T consent decree and four days of hearings on the oil pipeline consent decree.

The subcommittee experienced what it viewed as a lack of cooperation from the Department throughout its investigation, stating that "[t]he extent to which the Department of Justice went to withhold information from the committee in this investigation is unparalleled in the committee's experience." Consent Decree Report at xiii. With respect to the AT and T consent decree, DOJ unconditionally refused to make available to the subcommittee information from its files of that case. The subcommittee's chairman initially had written the Attorney General, requesting that he make available "all files in the Department of Justice relating to the negotiations for, and signing of, a consent decree in this case." Consent Decree Hearings at 1674.

Deputy Attorney General William P. Rogers asserted two grounds to support the Department's refusal to provide the subcommittee with such access. First, that the files contained information voluntarily submitted by AT and T in the course of consent decree negotiations. Rogers wrote the subcommittee chairman that "[w]ere [the files] made available to your subcommittee, this Department would violate the confidential nature of settlement negotiations and, in the process, discourage defendants, present and future, from entering into such negotiations." *Id.* at 1674-75. In a later letter, the head of the Antitrust Division, Victor Hansen, added that "[t]hose considerations which require that the Department treat on a confidential basis communications with a defendant during consent decree negotiations also apply to the enforcement of a decree." *Id.* at 3706.

The second reason given by Rogers for the Department's refusal to provide the subcommittee access to the AT and T files was that they contained memoranda and recommendations prepared by staff of the Antitrust Division, and the "essential process of full and flexible exchange might be seriously endangered were staff members hampered by the knowledge they might at some later date be forced to explain before Congress intermediate positions taken." *Id.* at 1675. Rogers stated that this action was being taken in accordance with an earlier directive from the President to the Department to that effect, which provided:

> Because it is essential to efficient and effective administration that employees of the executive branch be in a position to be completely candid in advising with each other on official matters, and because it is not in the public interest that any of their conversations or communications, or any documents or reproductions, concerning such advice be disclosed, you will instruct employees of your Department that in all of their appearances before [congressional] committees not to testify to any such conversations or communications or to produce any such document or reproductions. This principle must be maintained regardless of who would be benefitted by such disclosures.
>
> *Id.*

The subcommittee in its final report asserted that initially the "Attorney General refused access to the files of the Department of Justice primarily in order to prevent disclosure of facts that might prove embarrassing to the Department." Consent Decree Report at 42. The subcommittee further concluded that such withholding had "materially hampered the committee's investigation." However, it may be noted that the subcommittee was ultimately able to obtain much of the material concerning the AT and T consent decree that DOJ refused to provide directly from AT and T itself. *Id.*

The Department was, however, somewhat more forthcoming in permitting testimony of its attorneys about the AT and T consent decree. For example, the head of the Antitrust Division instructed two Division attorneys who had dissented from the decision to enter into the AT and T consent decree and had been called to testify before the subcommittee that "we do not at the present time think it appropriate...to...assert any privilege on behalf of the Department with regard to any information within [your] knowledge which is relevant to the negotiations of the decree in the Western Electric case." Consent Decree Hearings at 3647. These two attorneys later testified about those negotiations, including their reasons for differing with the Department's decision to enter into the consent decree. *Id.* at 3711-44.

COINTELPRO AND RELATED INVESTIGATIONS OF FBI-DOJ MISCONDUCT

Over the period 1974-1978, Senate and House committees examined the intelligence operations of a number of federal agencies, including the domestic intelligence operations of the FBI and various units of the Justice Department such as the Interdivision Information Unit. See S. Rep. No.755,

Books 1-3, 94th Cong., 2d Sess. (1976)(hereafter "Senate Intelligence Report"); Intelligence Activities, Senate Resolution 21: Hearings Before the Senate Select Comm. to Study Governmental Operations with Respect to Intelligence Activities, vols. 1-6, 94th Cong., 1st Sess. (1975)(hereafter "Senate Intelligence Hearings"); FBI Oversight: Hearings Before the Subcomm. on Civil and Constitutional Rights of the House Comm. of the Judiciary, parts 1-3, 94th Cong., 1st and 2d Sess. (1975-1976), parl;s 1-2, 95th Cong., 1st and 2d Sess. (1978)(hereafter "House FBI Hearings"). A select Senate committee examined 800 witnesses: 50 in public session, 250 in executive sessions and the balance in interviews. Senate Intelligence Report, Book II, at ix n.7. A number of those providing public testimony were present and former officials of the FBI and the Department of Justice.

The Select Committee estimated that in the course of its investigation it had obtained from these intelligence agencies and other sources approximately 110,000 pages of documents (still more were preliminarily reviewed at the agencies). *Id.* Hundreds of FBI documents were reprinted as hearing exhibits, though "[u]nder criteria determined by the Committee, in consultation with the Federal Bureau of Investigation, certain materials have been deleted from these exhibits to maintain the integrity of the internal operating procedures of the FBI. Further deletions were made with respect to protecting the privacy of certain individuals and groups. These deletions do not change the material content of these exhibits." Senate Intelligence Hearings at iv n.1. The select committee concluded in its final report that the "most important lesson" learned from its investigation was that "effective oversight is impossible without regular access to the underlying working documents of the intelligence community. Top level briefings do not adequately describe the realities. For that the documents are a necessary supplement and at times the only source." Senate Intelligence Report, Book II, ix n. 7.

Hearings on FBI domestic intelligence operations also were held before the House Judiciary Subcommittee on Civil and Constitutional Rights beginning in 1975. A number of Department of Justice and FBI officials testified, including Attorneys General Levi and Bell and FBI Director Kelly. At the request of the Chairman of the Judiciary Committee, the General Accounting Office in 1974 began a review of FBI operations in this area. FBI Oversight Hearings (94th Congress), part 2, at 1-2. In an attempt to analyze current FBI practices, the GAO chose ten FBI offices involved in varying levels of domestic intelligence activity, and randomly selected for review 899 cases (ultimately reduced to 797) in those offices that were acted on that year. *Id.* at 3.

The FBI agreed to GAO's proposal to have FBI agents prepare a summary of the information contained in the files of each of the selected cases. These summaries described the information that led to opening the investigation, methods and sources of collecting of information for the case, instructions from FBI Headquarters, and a brief summary of each document in the file. After reviewing the summaries, GAO staff held interviews with the FBI agents involved with the cases, as well as the agents who prepared the summaries. *Id.* at 3-4.

These hearings were continued in 1977 to hear the results of a similar GAO review of the FBI's domestic intelligence operations under new domestic security guidelines established by the Attorney General in 1976. In its follow-up investigation, GAO reviewed 319 additional randomly selected cases. As in its earlier review, GAO utilized FBI case summaries followed by agent interviews. This time, however, the Department also granted GAO access to copies of selected documents for verification purposes, with the names of informers and other sensitive data excised. House FBI Oversight Hearings (95th Congress), part 1, at 103.

WHITE COLLAR CRIME IN THE OIL INDUSTRY

In 1979, joint hearings were held by the Subcommittee on Energy and Power of the House Committee on Interstate and Foreign Commerce and the Subcommittee on Crime of the House Judiciary Committee to conduct an inquiry into allegations of fraudulent pricing of fuel in the oil industry and the failure of the Department of Energy and DOJ to effectively investigate and prosecute alleged criminality. See, White Collar Crime in the Oil Industry: Joint Hearings before the Subcommittee on Energy and Power of the House Committee on Interstate and Foreign Commerce and the Subcommittee on Crime of the House Commerce on the Judiciary, 96th Cong., 1st Sess. (1979)(hereinafter "White Collar Crime Hearings"). During the course of the hearing, testimony and evidence were received in closed session regarding open cases in which indictments were pending and criminal proceedings were in progressing. The Chairman of the Subcommittee on Energy and Power remarked: "We know indictments are outstanding. We do not wish to interfere with rights of any parties to a fair trial. To this end we have scrupulously avoided any actions that might have affected the indictment of any party. In these hearings we will restrict our questions to the process and the general schemes to defraud and the failure of the Government to pursue these cases. Evidence and comments on specific cases must be left to the prosecutors in the cases they bring to trial." White Collar Crime Hearings at 2. DOJ's Deputy Attorney General, Criminal Division, praised the Chairmen and committee members for their discreet conduct of the hearings: "I would like to commend Chairman Conyers, Chairman Dingell, and all other members of the committee and staff for the sensitivity which they have shown during the course of these hearings to the fact that we have ongoing criminal investigations and proceedings, and the appropriate handling of the question in order not to interfere with those investigations and criminal trials." *Id.* at 134.

The committees requested access to declination memoranda and the Justice Department stated that it had no objection, except to request that the information not be made public unless the committees had a compelling need. During the course of the hearing a DOJ staff attorney testified in open session as to the reason for not going forward with a particular criminal prosecution. Although a civil prosecution of the same matter was then pending, DOJ agreed to supply the committees with documents leading to the decision not to prosecute. *Id.* at 156-57.

BILLY CARTER/LIBYA INVESTIGATION

A special subcommittee of the Senate Committee on the Judiciary was constituted in 1980 to investigate the activities of individuals representing the interests of foreign governments. Due to the short time frame which it was given to report its conclusions to the Senate, the subcommittee narrowed the focus of its inquiry to the activities of the President's brother, Billy Carter, on behalf of the Libyan government. See Inquiry into the Matter of Billy Carter and Libya: Hearings Before the Subcommittee to Investigate the Activities of Individuals Representing the Interests of Foreign Governments of the Senate Comm. on the Judiciary, vols. 1-111, 96th Cong., 2d Sess. (1980)(hereafter "Billy Carter Hearings"); Inquiry into the Matter of Billy Carter and Libya, S. Rep. No. 1015, 96th Cong., 2d Sess. (1980)(hereafter "Billy Carter Report"). A significant portion of this inquiry concerned the Department's handling of its investigation of the Billy Carter matter, in particular whether Attorney General Benjamin R. Civiletti had acted improperly in withholding certain intelligence information about Billy Carter's contacts with Libya from the attorneys in the Criminal Division responsible for the investigation, or had otherwise sought to influence the disposition of the case.

Although there was early disagreement as to the extent of the subcommittee's access to certain information from the White House, there was no attempt by the Department to limit access to its attorneys involved with the Billy Carter case. The subcommittee heard testimony from several representatives of the Department, including Attorney General Civiletti, the Assistant Attorney General in charge of the Criminal Division, Philip B. Heymann, and three of his assistants. These witnesses testified about the general structure of decisionmaking in the Department, the nature of the investigation of Billy Carter's Libyan ties, the Attorney General's failure to immediately communicate intelligence information concerning Billy Carter to the Criminal Division attorneys conducting the investigation, the decision to proceed civilly and not criminally against Carter, and the effect of various actions of the Attorney General and the White House on that prosecutorial decision. Billy Carter Hearings at 116-30, 683-1153. The subcommittee also took depositions from some of these witnesses. Pursuant to a Senate Resolution providing it with such power, subcommittee staff took 35 depositions, totaling 2,646 pages. *Id.* at 1741-42.

The subcommittee also was given access to documents from the Department's files on the Billy Carter case. The materials obtained included prosecutorial memoranda, correspondence between the Department and Billy Carter, the handwritten notes of the attorney in charge of the foreign agents registration unit of the Criminal Division, and FBI investigative reports and summaries of interviews with Billy Carter and his associates. *Id.* at 755-978. Not included in the public record were a number of classified documents, which were forwarded to and kept in the files of the Senate Intelligence Committee. These classified documents were available for examination by designated staff members of the subcommittee and the Intelligence Committee, and some of the documents were later used by the subcommittee in executive session.

UNDERCOVER LAW ENFORCEMENT ACTIVITIES (ABSCAM)

In 1982, the Senate established a select committee to study the law enforcement undercover activities of the FBI and other components of the Department of Justice. See Law Enforcement Undercover Activities: Hearings Before the Senate Select Comm. to Study Law Enforcement Undercover Activities of Components of the Department of Justice, 97th

Cong., 2d Sess. (1982)(hereafter "Abscam Hearings"); Final Report of the Senate Select Comm. to Study Undercover Activities of Components of the Department of Justice, S. Rep. No.682, 97th Cong., 2d Sess. (1982). Representatives from the Department, including FBI Director William Webster, testified generally about the history of undercover operations engaged in by the Department, their benefits and costs, and the policies governing the institution and supervision of such operations, including several sets of guidelines promulgated by the Attorney General. These witnesses also testified about Abscam and several other specific undercover operations conducted by the FBI and other units of the Department. Abscam Hearings at 10-85, 153-226, 255-559, 895-924, 1031-70.

In addition to the witnesses from the Department providing public testimony, committee staff conducted interviews with a number of present and former Department attorneys and FBI agents. Abscam Report at 8-10. Among those testifying or interviewed were several present and former members of the Department's Brooklyn Organized Crime Strike Force. The Department wrote the committee that it "does not normally permit Strike Force attorneys to testify before congressional committees [and] have traditionally resisted questioning of this kind because it tends to inhibit prosecutors from proceeding through their normal tasks free from the fear that they may be second-guessed, with the benefit of hindsight, long after they take actions and make difficult judgements in the course of their duties." *Id.* at 486. The Department, nevertheless, agreed to this testimony, "because of their value to you as fact witnesses and because you have assured us that they will be asked to testify solely as to matters of fact within their personal knowledge and not conclusions or matters of policy ." *Id.*

The most extensive focus of the committee's inquiry was on the FBI's Abscam operation, which lasted from early 1978 through January 1980, and resulted in the criminal conviction of one Senator, six Members of the House of Representatives, several local officials, and others. As part of this review, the subcommittee was "given access to almost all of the confidential documents generated during the covert stage of the undercover operation known as Abscam." *Id.* at; v. In all, the committee reviewed more than 20,000 pages of Abscam documents, as well as video and audio tapes and tape transcripts, *id.* at 9, provided under the terms of an elaborate access agreement negotiated with the Department.

Pursuant to the agreement, the subcommittee was provided copies of confidential Abscam materials other than grand jury materials barred from disclosure under Rule 6(e) of the Federal of Criminal Procedure without a court order and certain prosecutorial memoranda from the Abscam cases.

Under the agreement, the Department was also permitted to withhold from the committee documents that might compromise ongoing investigations or reveal sensitive sources or investigative techniques, though the Department was required to describe each such document withheld, explain the basis of the denial, and give the committee an opportunity to propose conditions under which the documents might be provided. The committee further agreed to a "pledge of confidentiality" under which it was permitted to use and publicly disclose information derived from the confidential documents and to state that the information came from Department files, but was prohibited from publicly identifying the specific documents from which the information was obtained. All confidential documents were kept in a secure room, with access limited to the committee's members, its two counsel, and several designated document custodians. See generally, *id.* at v, 472-84. Later, DOJ agreed to permit access to those materials by other committee attorneys as well.

In addition to the documents to which it was given direct access, the committee received extensive oral briefings, including direct quotations, on basic factual material from the prosecutorial memoranda that were withheld, as well as from documents prepared or compiled by the Department's Office of Professional Responsibility as part of an internal investigation of possible misconduct in the Abscam operations and prosecutions. *Id.* at v.

Under the general framework established by this agreement, there was considerable give and take between the committee and the Department as to the degree of access that would be provided to specific documents. For example, the committee's counsel had sought access to a report prepared in the Criminal Division on FBI undercover operations. Abscam Hearings at 514. The committee's chairman had also written the Attorney General requesting access to that report. Abscam Report at 485. An agreement was reached whereby the report could be examined by committee members or counsel at the Department and notes taken on its contents, but it could neither be copied or removed from the Department. *Id.* at 494. Committee counsel utilized this procedure, but the committee determined that such limited access made it impractical for its members to personally review the report, and the committee's chairman again wrote the Attorney General asking for release of a copy. *Id.* at 498. The Department ultimately agreed to provide a copy of the report to each member of the committee, with the understanding that the report would not be disseminated beyond the members of the committee and its counsel, no additional copies would be made, and the copies provided by the Department would be returned at the conclusion of the committee's work. *Id.* at 501.

Finally, the committee retained the right under the access agreement to seek unrestricted access to documents if it determined that the limited access set forth in the agreement was insufficient to permit it to effectively conduct its investigation. *Id.* at v.

A similar investigation was conducted by the House Judiciary Subcommittee on Civil and Constitutional Rights, which held a total of twenty-one hearings over a period of four years. See FBI Undercover Activities, Authorization; and H.R. 3232: Oversight Hearings Before the Subcomm. on Civil and Constitutional Rights of the House Comm. on the Judiciary, 98th Cong., 1st Sess. (1983); FBI Undercover Operations: Hearings Before the Subcomm. on Civil and Constitutional Rights of the House Comm. on the Judiciary, 97th Cong., 1st Sess. (1981); FBI Oversight: Hearings Before the Subcomm. on Civil and Constitutional Rights of the House Comm. on the Judiciary, 96th Cong., 1st and 2d Sess. (1979-80). The subcommittee examined in detail the FBI's Operation Corkscrew undercover operation, an investigation of alleged corruption in the Cleveland Municipal Court, with access to confidential Department documents provided to it under an agreement patterned after the access agreement negotiated by the Senate select committee. Subcomm. on Civil and Constitutional Rights of the House Comm. on the Judiciary, FBI Undercover Operations, 98th Cong., 2d Sess. 91-93 (Comm. Print 1984).

Investigation of Withholding of EPA Documents

One of the most prominent Congressional investigations of the Department grew out of the highly charged confrontation at the end of the 97th Congress concerning the refusal of Environmental Protection Agency Administrator Ann Gorsuch Burford, under orders from the President, to comply with a House subcommittee subpoena requiring the production of documentation about EPA's enforcement of the hazardous waste cleanup legislation. This dispute culminated in the House of Representatives' citation of Burford for contempt of Congress, the first head of an Executive Branch agency ever to have been so cited by a House of Congress. It also resulted in the filing of an unprecedented legal action by the Department, in the name of the United States, against the House of Representatives and a number of its officials to obtain a judicial declaration that Burford had acted lawfully in refusing to comply with the subpoena.

Ultimately, the lawsuit was dismissed, *U.S. v. House of Representatives,* 557 F. Supp. 150 (D.D.C. 1983), the documents were provided to Congress, and the contempt citation was dropped. However, a number of questions about the role of the Department during the controversy remained: whether the Department, not EPA, had made the decision to persuade the President to assert executive privilege; whether the Department had directed the United States Attorney for the District of Columbia not to present the contempt certification of Burford to the grand jury for prosecution and had made the decision to sue the House; and, generally, whether there was a conflict of interest in the Department's simultaneously advising the President, representing Burford, investigating alleged Executive branch wrongdoing, and enforcing the Congressional criminal contempt statute. These and related questions raised by the Department's actions were the subject of an investigation by the House Judiciary Committee beginning in early 1983. The committee issued a final report on its investigation in December 1985. See Report of the House Comm. on the Judiciary on Investigation of the Role of the Department of Justice in the Withholding of Environmental Protection Agency Documents from Congress in 1982-1983, H.Rept. 99-435, 99th Cong., 1st Sess (1985) ("EPA Withholding Report").

Although the Judiciary Committee ultimately was able to obtain access to virtually all of the documentation and other information it sought from the Department, in many respects this investigation proved as contentious as the earlier EPA controversy from which it arose. In its final report, the committee concluded that:

> [T]he Department of Justice, through many of the same senior officials who were most involved in the EPA controversy, consciously prevented the Judiciary Committee from obtaining information in the Department's possession that was essential to the Committee's inquiry into the Department's role in that controversy. Most notably, the Department deliberately, and without advising the Committee, withheld a massive volume of vital handwritten notes and chronologies for over one year. These materials, which the Department knew came within the Committee's February 1983 document request, contained the bulk of the relevant documentary information about the Department's activities outlined in this report and provided a basis for many of the Committee's findings.

EPA Withholding Report at 1163; *see* also 1234-38. Among the other abuses cited by the committee were the withholding of a number of other relevant documents until the committee had independently learned of their existence, *id.* at 1164, as well as materially "false and misleading" testimony before the committee by the head of the Department's Office of Legal Counsel, *id.* at 1164-65 and 1191-1231.

The committee's initial request for documentation was contained in a February 1983 letter from its chairman, Peter Rodino, to Attorney General William French Smith. The committee requested the Department to "supply all documents prepared by or in the possession of the Department in any way relating to the withholding of documents that Congressional committees have subpoenaed from the EPA." *Id.* at 1167 and 1182-83. The letter also specifically requested, among other things, a narrative description of the activities of each division or other unit of the Department relating to the withholding of the EPA materials, information about the Department's apparent conflict of interest in simultaneously advising the Executive Branch while being responsible for prosecuting the Burford contempt citation, and any instructions given by the Department to the United States Attorney for the District of Columbia not to present the Burford contempt to the grand jury.

At first the Department provided only publicly available documents in response to this and other document requests of the committee. *Id.* at 1184. However, after a series of meetings between committee staff and senior Department officials, an agreement was reached whereby committee staff were permitted to review the materials responsive to these requests at the Department to determine which documents the committee would need for its inquiry. *Id.* at 1168 and 1233. Committee staff reviewed thousands of documents from the Land and Natural Resources Division, the Civil Division, the Office of Legal Counsel, the Office of Legislative Affairs, the Office of Public Affairs, and the offices of the Attorney General, the Deputy Attorney General, and the Solicitor General. *Id.* at 1168.

In July 1983, the committee chairman wrote to the Attorney General requesting copies of 105 documents that committee staff had identified in its review as particularly important to the committee's inquiry. *Id.* at 1169. By May 1984, only a few of those documents had been provided to the committee, and the chairman again wrote to the Attorney General requesting the Department's cooperation in the investigation. In that letter, the chairman advised the Attorney General that the committee's preliminary investigation had raised serious questions of misconduct, including potential criminal misconduct, in the actions of the Department in the withholding of the EPA documents. *Id.* at 1172. The committee finally received all of the 105 documents in July 1984, a full year after it had initially requested access. The committee at that time also obtained the written notes and a number of other documents that had been earlier withheld. *Id.* at 1173.

There was also disagreement about the access that would be provided to Department employees for interviews with committee staff. The Department demanded that it be permitted to have one or more Department attorneys present at each interview. The committee feared that the presence of Department representatives might intimidate the Department employees in their interviews and stated that it was willing to permit a Department representative to be present only if the representative was "walled-off" from Department officials involved with the controversy, if the substance of interviews was not revealed to subsequent interviewees, and if employees could be interviewed without a Department representative present if so requested. The Department ultimately agreed to permit the interviews to go forward without its attorneys present. If a Department employee requested representation, the Department employed private counsel for that purpose. In all, committee staff interviewed twenty-six current and former Department employees, including four Assistant Attorney Generals, under this agreement. *Id.* at 1174-76.

Partly as a result of these interviews, as well as from information in the handwritten notes that had been initially withheld, the committee concluded that it also required access to Criminal Division documents concerning the origins of the criminal investigation of former EPA Assistant Administrator Rita Lavelle in order to determine if the Department had considered instituting the investigation to obstruct the committee's inquiry. The committee also requested information about the Department's earlier withholding of the handwritten notes and other documents to determine whether Department officials had deliberately withheld the documents in an attempt to obstruct the committee's Investigation. *Id.* at 1176-77 and 1263-64. The Department at first refused to provide the committee with documents relating to its Lavelle investigation "[c]onsistent with the longstanding practice of the Department not to provide access to active criminal files." *Id.* at 1265. The Department also refused to provide the committee with access to documentation related to the Department's handling of the committee's inquiry, objecting to the committee's "ever- broadening scope of ...inquiry." *Id.* at 1265.

The committee chairman wrote the Attorney General and objected that the Department was denying the committee access even though no claim of executive privilege had been asserted. *Id.* at 1266. The chairman also maintained that "[i]n this case, of course, no claim of executive privilege could lie because of the interest of the committee in determining whether the documents contain evidence of misconduct by executive branch officials." *Id.* With respect to the documents relating to the Department's handling of the committee inquiry, the chairman demanded that the Department prepare a detailed index of the withheld documents, including the title, date, and length of each document, its author and all who had seen it, a summary of its contents, an explanation of why it was being withheld, and a certification that the Department intended to recommend to the President the assertion of executive privilege as to each withheld document and that each document contained no evidence of misconduct. *Id.* at 1268-69. With respect to the Lavelle documents, the chairman narrowed the committee's request to "predicate" documents relating to the opening of the investigation and prosecution of Lavelle, as opposed to FBI and other investigative reports reflecting actual investigative work conducted after the opening of the investigation. *Id.* at 1269-70. In response, after a period of more than three months from the committee's initial request, the Department produced those two categories of materials. *Id.* at 1270.

E.F. HUTTON INVESTIGATION

In 1985 and 1986, the Crime Subcommittee of the House Judiciary Committee conducted an investigation to determine why no individuals were charged in connection with an investigation of E.F. Hutton in which the company pled guilty to 2,000 felony counts. See, E.F. Hutton Mail and Wire Fraud, Report of the House Subcommittee on Crime, Committee on the Judiciary, 99th Cong. 2d Sess. (Committee Print, Serial No. 13, December 1986) (Hutton Report). As part of this investigation, the subcommittee sought letters to Hutton employees promising not to prosecute, draft indictments, and internal DOJ communications regarding proposals by or within the Justice Department regarding the disposition of charges against Hutton employees. Hutton Report at 1119. Assistant Attorney General Trott responded to the request by stating:

> We understand this to be a request for prospective memoranda ... It now appears that there is one document prepared early in the investigation that may fall within your request. We will produce that for the Subcommittee after appropriate redactions have been made. We believe that the necessary redactions are those principally set out in *In re Grand Jury Investigation(Lance)*, 610 F. 2d 202, 216-17 (5th Cir. 1080) (opinions or statement based on knowledge of grand jury proceedings may be disclosed "provided, of course, the statement does not reveal the grand jury information on which it is based.") Thus, such information as the identity of witnesses who testified before the grand jury and the substance of their

testimony and the identity of documents which were subpoenaed by the grand jury must be redacted." Hutton Report at 1217.

The Justice Department also recommended that the subcommittee go to court to obtain access to all of the information, including that covered by Rule 6(e). Hutton Report at 1218. The Justice Department went to court to seek guidance regarding the applicability of Rule 6(e) to the documents sought by the subcommittee. In court, the Justice Department argued only on 6(e) grounds, and never claimed that any documents should be withheld on deliberative process grounds. The court dismissed the case because it presented no case or controversy. However, the court expressed "serious doubt" as to the applicability of Rule 6(e) to the documents sought by the subcommittee.

The Subcommittee report includes as exhibits a number of deliberative prosecutorial documents. One 21-page memorandum contains a detailed discussion of Hutton's money management practices, and concludes "these money management techniques violated numerous federal criminal statutes and, therefore, prosecution is appropriate and recommended." (See Hutton Report at 1328.) The committee was also provided with a series of memoranda prepared by a line attorney which analyzed the defenses which could be offered by Hutton officers, and the DOJ's responses to those defenses. These memoranda are among many examples of deliberative prosecutorial memoranda provided by DOJ. *See* Hutton Report 1329-35.

IRAN-CONTRA

In the late 1980s, an intense Congressional investigation focused, in part, on Attorney General Meese's conduct during the Iran-Contra scandal. The House and Senate created their Iran-Contra committees in January, 1987. The Iran-Contra committees demanded the production of the Justice Department's files, to which Assistant Attorney General John Bolton responded, on behalf of Attorney General Meese, by attempting to withhold the documents on the claim that providing them would prejudice the pending or anticipated litigation by the Independent Counsel. The Iran-Contra committees disputed that contention, required the furnishing of all Justice Department documents, and questioned all knowledgeable Justice Department officers up to, and including, Attorney General Meese.

One major aspect of the Iran-Contra Committees' investigation focused on the inadequacies of the so-called "Meese Inquiry," the team led by

Attorney General Meese which looked into the National Security Council (NSC) staff in late November, 1987. The Iran-Contra committees concluded, that this inquiry had the effect of forwarning the NSC staff to shred their records and fix upon an agreed false story, and by the Meese team's methods the last vital opportunity to uncover the obscured aspects of the scandal was foreclosed. The Congressional investigation provided documentary evidence regarding incompetence, at best, by the Attorney General's inquiry team during the Meese Inquiry. The Congressional report summed up such matters as the Attorney General's taking no notes and remembering no details of his crucial interviews of CIA Director Casey and others, the Justice Department inquiry's not taking any steps to secure the remaining unshredded documents, and the Justice Department team's allowing the shredding to occur while the team was in the room; the inquiry team excluded the Criminal Division and the FBI from the case until it was too late. According to the Congressional report the Attorney General gave his press conference of November 25, 1986, with an account that in key respects misstated and concealed embarrassing information which had been furnished to him. See, Report of the Congressional Committees Investigating the Iran-Contra Affair, H.R. Rep. No.433 and S. Rep. No.216, 100th Cong., 1st Sess. 310, 317, 314, 317-18, 647 (1987).

Rocky Flats Environmental Crimes Plea Bargain

In June 1992 the Subcommittee on Investigations and Oversight of the House Committee on Science, Space, and Technology commenced a review of the plea bargain settlement by the Department of Justice of the government's investigation and prosecution of environmental crimes committed by Rockwell International Corporation in its capacity as manager and operating contractor at the Department of Energy's (DOE) Rocky Flats nuclear weapons facility. See Environmental Crimes at the Rocky Flats Nuclear Weapons Facility: Hearings Before the Subcomm. on Investigations and Oversight of the House Committee on Science, Space and Technology, 102d Cong., 2d Sess., Vols. I and II (1992) ("Rocky Flats Hearings"); Meetings: To Subpoena Appearance by Employees of the Department of Justice and the FBI and To Subpoena Production of Documents From Rockwell International Corporation, Before the Subcomm. on Investigations and Oversight of the House Comm. on Science, Space, and Technology, 102d Congress, 2d Sess., (1992)("Subpoena Meetings").

The settlement was a culmination of a five-year investigation of environmental crimes at the facility, conducted by a joint government task force involving the FBI, the Department of Justice, the Environmental Protection Agency (EPA), EPA's National Enforcement Investigation Centers, and the DOE Inspector General. The subcommittee was concerned with the size of the fine agreed to relative to the profits made by the contractor and the damage caused by inappropriate activities; the lack of personal indictments of either Rockwell or DOE personnel despite a DOJ finding that the crimes were "institutional crimes" that "were the result of a culture, substantially encouraged and nurtured by DOE, where environmental compliance was a much lower priority than the production and recovery of plutonium and the manufacture of nuclear 'triggers'"; and that reimbursements provided by the government to Rockwell for expenses in the cases and the contractual arrangements between Rockwell and DOE may have created disincentives for environmental compliance and aggressive prosecution of the case.

The subcommittee held ten days of hearings, seven in executive session, in which it took testimony from the United States Attorney for the District of Colorado; an assistant U .S. Attorney for the District of Colorado; a DOJ line attorney from Main Justice; and an FBI field agent; and received voluminous FBI field investigative reports and interview summaries, and documents submitted to the grand jury not subject to Rule 6(e). Rocky Flats Hearing, Vol. I, at 389-1009, 1111-1251; Vol. II.

At one point in the proceedings all the witnesses who were under subpoena, upon written instructions from the Acting Assistant Attorney General, Criminal Division, refused to answer questions concerning internal deliberations in which decisions were made about the investigation and prosecution of Rockwell, the DOE and their employees. Two of the witnesses advised that they had information and, but for the DOJ directive, would have answered the subcommittee's inquiries. The subcommittee members unanimously authorized the chairman to send a letter to President G. H. W. Bush requesting that he either personally assert executive privilege as the basis for directing the witnesses to withhold the information or direct DOJ to retract its instructions to the witnesses. The President took neither course and the DOJ subsequently reiterated its position that the matter sought would chill Department personnel. The subcommittee then moved to hold the U .S. Attorney in contempt of Congress.

A last minute agreement forestalled the contempt citation. Under the agreement (1) DOJ issued a new instruction to all personnel under subpoena to answer all questions put to them by the subcommittee, including those which related to internal deliberations with respect to the plea bargain. Those instructions were to apply as well to all Department witnesses, including FBI personnel, who might be called in the future. (2) Transcripts were to be made of all interviews and provided to the witnesses. They were not to be made public except to the extent they needed to be used to refresh the recollection or impeach the testimony of other witnesses called before the subcommittee in a public hearing. (3) Witnesses were to be interviewed by staff under oath. (4) The subcommittee reserved the right to hold further hearings in the future at which time it could call other Department witnesses who would be instructed not to invoke the deliberative process privilege as a reason for not answering subcommittee questions. Rocky Flats Hearings, Vol. I at 9-10, 25-31,1673-1737; Subpoena Hearings, at 1-3, 82-86, 143-51.

INVESTIGATION OF THE JUSTICE DEPARTMENT'S ENVIRONMENTAL CRIMES SECTION

From 1992 to 1994, the House Commerce Committee's Subcommittee on Oversight and Investigations conducted an extensive investigation into the impact of the Department of Justice (DOJ) on the effectiveness of the Environmental Protection Agency's (EPA) criminal enforcement program. The probe involved two public hearings, nearly three years of staff work, intensive review of documents (many of which were obtained only though subpoenas), and the effort to overcome persistent Department resistance. The investigation focused on allegations of mismanagement of the Environmental Crimes Section (ECS), the DOJ Headquarters component charged with environmental prosecution responsibilities; and the effect on the relationship between U.S. Attorneys' offices and the ECS as a consequence of Main Justice's decision to centralize control of environmental prosecution in Washington, D.C. at the very same time that all other areas of prosecution control were being decentralized.

The Subcommittee's investigation was delayed for months by DOJ refusals of requests to interview DOJ line attorneys and the denial of access to numerous primary decisionmaking documents as well as documents prepared in response to the Subcommittee's investigation. The initial phase of the investigation required overcoming refusals to produce internal EPA documents bearing on 17 closed criminal environmental cases. The documents ultimately produced by EPA included Reports of Investigation, case agent notes, internal reports and memoranda, communications with private parties, and correspondence with DOJ. The next phase concentrated on attempts to obtain staff interviews with DOJ line attorneys with first hand information on whether various closed cases had been mishandled, including three Assistant United States Attorneys. DOJ officials initially refused on the ground of the chilling effect such access would have and the historic reluctance of the Department to allow such access, offering instead to provide access to the head of ECS instead. The Subcommittee responded that it was premature to interview the ECS head without interviewing line attorneys who had first hand knowledge of the facts in question. The change of administration in 1993 did not result in an easing of DOJ's resistant posture and in May 1993 the Subcommittee voted to issue 26 subpoenas to present and former DOJ attorneys. In June 1993 DOJ acquiesced to staff interviews of the subpoenaed attorneys pursuant to a negotiated agreement. Document subpoenas were also authorized but not issued. However, continued refusal to voluntarily produce the documents resulted in their issuance and service in March 1994 on the Attorney General and the Acting Assistant Attorney General for the Environment and Natural Resources Division. Some of these documents involved closed cases, but DOJ claimed they were "deliberative" in nature and that only limited access could be allowed for them. Other documents withheld involved internal DOJ communications respecting responses to the Subcommittee's investigation after the six cases were closed. At the time the subpoenas were served, the Acting Assistant Attorney General's nomination for the position was before the Senate Judiciary Committee. The Chairman of the Subcommittee advised the Judiciary Committee of the withholding and a hold was put on her nomination. In late March, DOJ agreed to comply with the subpoena and the documents were provided over a period of months. Coincidentally the Senate hold was lifted.

The major results of the investigation and its revelations were the reversal of the policy of centralization of control of environmental prosecutions in Washington, D.C., and the return of such control to the U.S. Attorney's offices; and the replacement of the top management of the ECS. See "Damaging Disarray: Organizational Breakdown and Reform in the Justice Department's Environmental Crimes Program," 103d Cong., 2d Sess. 1-4, 10-40 (1994)(Comm. Print #103-T).

Campaign Finance Investigations

Allegations of violations of campaign finance laws and regulations surfaced during the latter stages of the 1996 presidential election campaign and became objects of investigations by committees in both Houses between 1996 and 2000. Several of the committee inquiries focused on the nature and propriety of DOJ actions and non-actions during the course of investigations undertaken by the Department. Two are illustrative.

In 1997, the Senate Governmental Affairs Committee began an investigation into allegations of improprieties with respect to the flow of money into campaigns, particularly into the Republican and Democratic National Committees, and especially with respect to money from foreign sources. After the first round of hearings, the committee became concerned with the quality of DOJ's prosecution efforts as well as with evidence of a lack of cooperation and coordination between Main Justice and the FBI. In 1999 the committee held hearings on DOJ's handling of the investigation of Yah Lin "Charlie" Trie, a person from Arkansas with a long time friendly relationship with President Clinton, who had frequent access to the White House and was alleged to have funneled $220,000 from foreign sources to the Democratic National Committee. Mr. Trie also provided the President's Legal Expense Trust (PLET) with $789,000 in sequentially numbered money orders. During the course of the DOJ investigation, Mr. Trie fled the country, leaving an agent in control of his business. In April 1997, the committee subpoenaed business documents relating to its campaign finance investigation and documents relating to the PLET. At the same time the DOJ's Campaign Finance Task Force was engaged in a parallel investigation. As early as June 1997 FBI Agents in Little Rock became convinced that Trie's agent was destroying subpoenaed documents, a process that continued until October 1997. During that period the FBI attempted to obtain a search warrant to prevent further document destruction. DOJ Task Force supervisory attorneys declined to grant permission to seek a search warrant on the ground there was insufficient probable cause. The committee subpoenaed four FBI special agents who testified to their efforts to procure a search warrant, as well as the Task Force supervisory attorney who refused its issuance and the Chief of the Public Integrity Section of DOJ. The committee also obtained from DOJ the investigatory notes of the special agents, the draft affidavit in support of the warrant requests, the notes of the Task Force supervisor, and a memo from one of the special agents to FBI Director Freeh expressing concern over DOJ handling of the investigation. See, Hearing, The Justice Department's Handling of the Yah Lin "Charlie"

Trie Case, before the Senate Committee on Governmental Affairs, 106th Cong., 1st Sess. 3-4, 14-63, 105-133 (1999).

In December 1997, press reports indicated that FBI Director Freeh had sent a memorandum to Attorney General Reno suggesting that she seek appointment of an independent counsel to conduct the campaign finance investigation in order to avoid an appearance of a political conflict of interest. The House Committee on Government Reform and Oversight scheduled a hearing and requested that Freeh appear and produce the memo. The Attorney General intervened and explained that she would not comply on the grounds of the longstanding DOJ policy prohibiting sharing of deliberative material in open criminal cases with the Congress, and to prevent the chilling effect such disclosures would have on Department personnel in future investigations. The committee issued subpoenas on December 5, 1997 and both Reno and Freeh refused to comply. At no time did the Attorney General make a claim of executive privilege. In July 1998 the committee learned that the head of DOJ's Campaign Finance Task Force, Charles La Bella, had prepared a lengthy memorandum for the Attorney General which concluded that the Attorney General was required by both the mandatory and discretionary provisions of the independent counsel law to appoint an independent counsel. On July 24, 1998, the committee issued a subpoena for both the Freeh and La Bella memos. The Attorney General refused compliance again and on August 6, 1998, the committee voted to hold the Attorney General in contempt of Congress. See Contempt of Congress, Report of the Committee on Government Reform and Oversight on the Refusal of Attorney General Janet Reno to Produce Documents Subpoenaed by the Government Reform and Oversight Committee, H. Rept. No. 105-728, 105th Cong., 2d Sess. (1998). However, the contempt report was not taken up on the House floor prior to the end of the 105th Congress.

On March 10, 2000, following press reports indicating that the La Bella memo had been leaked in its entirety to a newspaper, the committee again subpoenaed the memos. The Attorney General still refused to release the memos but offered to allow committee staff unredacted review but without any note taking. Negotiations continued but the committee began review under the DOJ conditions. Ultimately, an accommodation was reached in which all memoranda subject to subpoena were to be produced to the committee. The documents would be kept in a secure facility with access restricted to a limited number staff. The committee agreed to give DOJ notice in advance of its intent to release the documents and to allow DOJ the opportunity to explain why they should not be disclosed. The committee notified the Attorney General of its intent to release the documents at a June

6 hearing. The memos were released to the public on that date by unanimous consent.

Misuse of Informants in the FBI's Boston Regional Office

In early 2001, the House Committee on Government Reform commenced an investigation on FBI corruption in its Boston Regional office that encompassed events that extended back to the mid-1960's. After repeated instances of lack of cooperation with requests for documents, the committee issued a subpoena on September 6, 2001, for a number of prosecution and declination memoranda relating to its investigation of the handling of a confidential informants in New England. DOJ officials made it clear that it would not comply. In December 2001 the committee renewed its request for the subpoenaed documents. (A hearing on the request scheduled for September 13, 2001 had been postponed because of the September 11 terrorist attacks.) That subpoena sought, among other material, Justice Department documents relating to alleged law enforcement corruption in the Federal Bureau of Investigation's Boston office that occurred over a period of almost 30 years. During that time, FBI officials allegedly knowingly allowed innocent persons to be convicted of murder on the false testimony of a cooperating witness and two informants in order to protect the undercover activities of those informants. Later, the FBI knowingly permitted two other informants to commit some 21 additional murders during the period they acted as informants, and, finally, gave the informants warning of an impending grand jury indictment which allowed one of them to flee.

The President directed the Attorney General not to release the documents because disclosure "would inhibit the candor necessary to the effectiveness of the deliberative processes by which the Department makes prosecutorial decisions," and that committee access to the documents "threatens to politicize the criminal justice process" and to undermine the fundamental purpose of the separation of power doctrine, "which was to protect individual liberty." In defending the assertion of the privilege the Justice Department claimed a historical policy of withholding deliberative prosecutorial documents from Congress in both open and closed civil and criminal cases. See, Louis Fisher, "The Politics of Executive Privilege," Carolina Academic Press, 108 (2004)(Fisher). Pending at the time were a number of Federal Tort Claims Act suits brought by the falsely convicted persons and their families, claiming the government knowingly used fabricated testimony to achieve the conviction.

Initial congressional hearings after the privilege claim was made demonstrated the rigidity of the Department's position. The Department later agreed there might be some area for compromise, and on January 10, 2002, White House Counsel Gonzales wrote to Chairman Burton conceding that it was a "misimpression" that congressional committees could never have access to deliberative documents from a criminal investigation or prosecution. "There is no such bright-line policy, nor did we intend to articulate any such policy." But, he continued, since the documents "sought a very narrow and particularly sensitive category of deliberative matters" and "absent unusual circumstances, the Executive Branch has traditionally protected these highly sensitive deliberative documents against public or congressional disclosure" unless a committee showed a "compelling or specific need" for the documents. See, Fisher, *id.* The documents continued to be withheld until a further hearing, held on February 6, 2002, when the committee heard expert testimony describing over 30 specific instances since 1920 of the Department of Justice giving access to prosecutorial memoranda for both open and closed cases and providing testimony of subordinate Department employees, such as line attorneys, FBI field agents and U.S. attorneys, and included detailed testimony about specific instances of DOJ's failure to prosecute meritorious cases. In all instances, investigating committees were provided with documents respecting open and closed cases that often included prosecutorial memoranda, FBI investigative reports, summaries of FBI interviews, memoranda and correspondence prepared during undercover operations, and documents presented to grand juries not protected by Rule 6(e), among other similar "sensitive materials." Shortly after the hearing the committee was given access to the disputed documents."Everything Secret Degenerates: The FBI's Use of Murderers As Informants," H.Rept. 108-414, 108th Cong., 2d Sess. 2-9, 121-134 (2004) (House Report); Hearings, " Investigation Into Allegations of Justice Department Misconduct In New England-Volume I," House Comm. on Government Reform, 107th Cong., 1st and 2d Sess's. 520-556, 562-604 (May 3, December 13, 2001; February 6, 2002) (Hearings); *McIntyre v. United States*, 367 F.3d 38, 42-51 (1st Cir. 2004)(recounting background of FBI corrupt activities); *United States v. Salemme*, 91 F. Supp. 2d 141, 148-63, 208-15, 322 (D.Mass. 1993) (same); *United States v. Flemmi,* 195 F. Supp 243, 249-50 (D. Mass. 200) (same); Charles Tiefer, "President Bush's First Executive Privilege Claim: The FBI/Boston Investigation," 33 Pres. Stud. Q. 201(2003). On July 26, 2007, a Massachusetts federal district court judge awarded the convicted persons and their families $101.7 million under the Federal Tort Claims Act, finding the government liable for malicious prosecution, civil conspiracy, infliction of emotional distress, and negligence. Shelly Murphy and Brian R. Ballou, "FBI Condemned in Landmark Ruling," Boston Globe, July 27, 2007, A3; Robert Barrens and Paul Lewis, "FBI Must Pay $102 Million In Mob Case," Washington Post, July 27, 2007, A3.

The committee's final report concluded that the documents withheld from it were indispensable to the success of its investigation and that the claim of presidential privilege was part of a pattern of obstruction that impeded its investigation:

> When the FBI Office of Professional Responsibility conducted an investigation of the activities of New England law enforcement, it concluded in 1997: "There is no evidence that prosecutorial discretion was exercised on behalf of informants [James] Bulger and/or [Stephen] Flemmi." This is untrue. Former U.S. Attorney Jeremiah O'Sullivan was asked in the December 5, 2002 committee hearing whether prosecutorial discretion had been exercised on behalf of Bulger and Flemmi and he said that it had. A review of documents in the possession of the Justice Department also confirms this to be true. Had the committee permitted the assertion of executive privilege by the President to be unchallenged, this information would never have been known. That the Justice Department concluded that prosecutorial discretion had not benefitted Bulger or Flemmi —while at the same time fighting to keep Congress from obtaining information proving this statement to be untrue — is extremely troubling. See, House Report at 3, 134-135.

REMOVAL AND REPLACEMENT OF UNITED STATES ATTORNEYS

Commencing in early 2007, the House Judiciary Committee and its Subcommittee on Commercial and Administrative Law and the Senate Judiciary Committee began investigations of the termination and replacement of nine United States Attorneys in 2006; The committees sought an explanation of the reasons for the terminations, who was involved in the removal and replacement decisions, and what factors may have influenced the considerations for removal and replacement. During the initial phase of the investigations DOJ voluntarily provided former and current Department officials and employees for closed door interviews and testimony at hearings. The House subcommittee held five days of hearings, on March 6, March 29, May 3, June 21, and July 12, 2007. The full committee held two days of hearings, on May 10 and May 23, 2007. DOJ personnel provided included, among others, the Attorney General; the Deputy Attorney General; the removed Untied States Attorneys; the Chief of Staff to the Deputy Attorney General; the former Chief of Staff to the Attorney General; the acting Associate Attorney General; the Principal Associate Deputy Attorney General; the Deputy Assistant Attorney General and Chief of Staff of the Criminal Division; the Principal Deputy Director of the Executive Office of U.S. Attorneys; the former Director of the Office of U.S. Attorneys and current U.S. Attorney for the Western District of Pennsylvania; the Associate Deputy Attorney General; and the Acting Attorney General for New Mexico.

On the basis of the testimony of the witnesses and records produced by them and DOJ, the committees turned their attention to the role the White House played in the removals and sought similar voluntary provision of witnesses and documents. The White House Counsel responded with a proposal under which the committees were offered limited availability to some documents and limited access to witnesses in closed sessions, but without any transcripts of the interviews and under limitation as to permissible areas of questions. Also, as a condition of this proposal the committees had to commit in advance not to subsequently pursue any additional White House-related information by any other means, regardless of whatever the initial review of documents should reveal.

Upon the failure to procure White House documents and witnesses on a voluntary basis, on June 13, 2007 the chairman of the House and Senate committee issued subpoenas to Joshua Bolten, the White House Chief of Staff (as custodian of the White House Documents) for relevant White House documents, returnable on June 28, 2007. On that date, the House committee chairman issued a subpoena for documents and testimony to former White House Counsel Harriet Meirs, returnable on July 12, 2007; and the Senate committee chairman issued a similar subpoena to former White House Political Director Sara Taylor, returnable on July 11, 2007. The White House Counsel thereafter announced that no documents would be produced by Mr. Bolten on the basis of a claim of Executive privilege by the President, and that no logs of the withheld documents would be provided; and that Ms. Miers had been directed to claim Executive privilege by the President and not to appear at the hearing at all based on the notion that the assertion of presidential privilege cloaked a witness with “absolute immunity” from even appearing in response to a subpoena. On the return dates of the subpoenas

Ms. Miers did not appear and Mr. Bolten did not supply the subpoenaed documents.

On July 12, the House subcommittee voted 7-5 to hold Miers in contempt of Congress, and on July 19, Bolten was held in contempt by the subcommittee by a 7-3 vote. On July 25 both Miers and Bolten were held in contempt by the full Judiciary Committee by a vote of 21-17. As of the date of this writing the resolution of contempt has not been acted upon by the House. See, "Resolution Recommending That The House of Representatives Find Harriet Miers and Joshua Bolten, Chief of Staff, White House In Contempt of Congress For Refusal to Comply With Subpoenas Duly Issued By the Committee on the Judiciary," 110th Cong. 1st Sess. (July 25, 2007) (with additional views); and CRS Report RL30319, *Presidential Claims of Executive Privilege: History, Law, Practice and Recent Developments*, by Morton Rosenberg.

REFERENCES

[1] See generally, CRS Report RL30240, *Congressional Oversight Manual*, 5-17, 87-108, 114-140 (Oversight Manual).

[2] Oversight Manual at 2-4.

[3] The subpoenaed documents in Burford I, discussed *infra* at 8-9, included "memoranda by Agency or Department of Justice attorneys containing litigation and negotiation strategy, settlement positions, and other similar material." H.Rept. 97-968, 97th Cong. 2d. Sess. 18, 28-29 (1982). The documents sought in the Boston FBI matter were all internal DOJ materials. See discussion *infra* at 14.

[4] *McGrain v. Daugherty,* 273 U.S. 135 (1927).

[5] 421 U.S. at 504, n. 15 (quoting *Barenblatt v. United States*, 360 U.S. 109, 111).

[6] 354 U.S. 178, 187 (1957).

[7] Id.

[8] *Id.* at 182.

[9] *Id.* at 194-195.

[10] *Id.* at 200 n. 33.

[11] 273 U.S. 135 (1927).

[12] 273 U.S. at 177-78.

[13] 279 U.S. 263 (1929).

[14] *Id.* at 290.

[15] *Id.* at 295.

[16] Id.

[17] *McGrain v. Daugherty,* 273 U.S. 135, 151 (1927).

[18] Investigation of Hon. Harry M. Daughtery, Formerly Attorney General of the United States: Hearings Before the Senate Select Committee on

Investigation of the Attorney General, vols. 1-3, 68th Congress, 1st Session (1924).

[19] See*, e.g., id.* at 1495-1503, 1529-30, 2295-96.

[20] *Id.* at 1120.

[21] *Id.* at 1078- 79.

[22] *Id.* at 1015-16 and 1159-60.

[23] *Id.* at 2389.

[24] *Id.* at 1495-1547.

[25] *Id.* at 1790.

[26] See H.Rept. 97- 968, 97th Cong. 2d Sess. (1982) [hereinafter House Report].

[27] House Report at 13-20.

[28] See 8 Op. O.L.C. 101, 107 (1984) [hereinafter 1984 OLC Opinion].

[29] See *United States v. U.S. Houses of Representatives,* 556 F.Supp. 150 (D.D.C. 1983): See *also,* 2 U.S.C. § 192, 194 (1980).

[30] See Memorandum of Understanding Between the Committee on Public Works and Transportation and the Department of Justice, Concerning Documents Subpoenaed from the Environmental Protection Agency, February 18, 1983; see *also* H. Rept. No. 323, 98th Cong., 1st Sess., 18-20 (1983) (copy on file with authors).

[31] See *EPA Document Agreement*, CQ WEEKLY REPORT, March 26, 1983 at 685 (copy on file with authors).

[32] Id.

[33] Id.

[34] Id.

[35] Id.

[36] Id.

[37] Id.

[38] See, Report of the House Comm. on the Judiciary on Investigation of the Role of the Department of Justice in the Withholding of Environmental Protection Agency Documents from Congress in 1982-1983, H.Rept. 99-435, 99th Cong., 1st Sess. (1985) ("EPA Withholding Report").

[39] EPA Withholding Report at 1163; *see* also 1234-38.

[40] *Id.* at 1164.

[41] *Id.* at 1164-65 and 1191-1231.

[42] *Id.* at 1167 and 1182-83.

[43] *Id.* at 1184.

[44] *Id.* at 1168 and 1233.

[45] *Id.* at 1168.

[46] *Id.* at 1169.
[47] *Id.* at 1172.
[48] *Id.* at 1173.
[49] *Id.* at 1174-76.
[50] *Id.* at 1176-77 and 1263-64.
[51] *Id.* at 1265.
[52] *Id.* at 1265.
[53] *Id.* at 1266.
[54] *Id.*
[55] *Id.* at 1268-69.
[56] *Id.* at 1269-70.
[57] *Id.* at 1270.
[58] See Environmental Crimes at the Rocky Flats Nuclear Weapons Facility: Hearings Before the Subcomm. on Investigations and Oversight of the House Committee on Science, Space and Technology, 102d Cong., 2d Sess., Vols. I and II (1992) ("Rocky Flats Hearings");Meetings: To Subpoena Appearance by Employees of the Department of Justice and the FBI and To Subpoena Production of Documents From Rockwell International Corporation, Before the Subcomm. on Investigations and Oversight of the House Comm. on Science, Space, and Technology, 102d Congress, 2d Sess., (1992)("Subpoena Meetings").
[59] Rocky Flats Hearing, Vol. I, at 389-1009, 1111-1251; Vol. II.
[60] Rocky Flats Hearings, Vol. I at 9-10,25-31,1673-1737; Subpoena Hearings, at 1-3, 82-86, 143-51.
[61] Louis Fisher, "The Politics of Executive Privilege," Carolina Academic Press, 108 (2004)(Fisher).
*[62]*Fisher, *Id.*
[63] "Everything Secret Degenerates: The FBI's Use of Murderers As Informants," H.Rept. 108-414, 108th Cong., 2d Sess. 2-9, 121-134 (2004)(House Report); Hearings, " Investigation Into Allegations of Justice Department Misconduct In New England-Volume I", House Comm. on Government Reform, 107th Cong., 1st and 2d Sess's. 520-556, 562-604 (May 3, December 13, 2001; February 6, 2002) (Hearings); *McIntyre v. United States*, 367 F.3d 38, 42-51 (1st Cir. 2004)(recounting background of FBI corrupt activities); *United States v. Salemme*, 91 F. Supp. 2d 141, 148-63, 208-15, 322 (D.Mass. 1993) (same); *United States v. Flemmi,* 195 F. Supp 243, 249-50 (D. Mass. 200); (same) Charles Tiefer, "President Bush's First Executive Privilege Claim: The FBI/Boston Investigation", 33 Pres. Stud. Q. 201(2003). On July 26,

2007, a Massachusetts federal district court judge awarded the convicted persons and their families $101.7 million under the Federal Tort Claims Act, finding the government liable of malicious prosecution, civil conspiracy, infliction of emotional distress, and negligence. Shelly Murphy and Brian R. Ballou, "FBI Condemned in Landmark Ruling," Boston Globe, July 27, 2007, A3; Robert Barrens and Paul Lewis, "FBI Must Pay $102 Million In Mob Case," Washington Post, July 27, 2007, A3.

[64] House Report at 3, 134-135.

[65] See Hearings, *supra*, at 549-50, 555.

[66] Hearings, "The Federal Raid on Ruby Ridge, Idaho," before the Senate Subcommittee on Terrorism, Technology, Government Information, Committee on the Judiciary, 104th Cong., 1st Sess. (1995) (Ruby Ridge Hearings).

[67] Ruby Ridge: Report of the Subcommittee on Terrorism, Technology and Government Information of the Senate Committee on the Judiciary (Ruby Ridge Report). The 154-page document appears not to have been officially reported by the full Committee. A bound copy may be found in the United States Senate Library, catalogue number HV 8141.U56 1995.

[68] Ruby Ridge Report at 1; Ruby Ridge Hearings at 722, 954, 961.

[69] The Task Force Report was never publically released or printed in the subcommittee's hearing record. A bound copy of the Report provided the subcommittee may be found in the United States Senate Library, catalogue number HV814.U55 1995.

[70] Weaver was convicted for failure to appear for a trial and for commission of an offense while on release.

[71] See, e.g., Ruby Ridge Hearings at 719-737, 941-985; Ruby Ridge Report at 10-11 ("With the exceptions of the [Ruby Ridge] Task Force Report, which was partially disavowed by the Department, and the April 5, 1995 memorandum of Deputy Attorney General Jamie Gorelick, it appeared to the subcommittee that the authors of every report we read were looking more to justify agency conduct than to follow the facts wherever they lead."), 61-69, 115, 122-23, 134-35, 139, 145-49.

[72] 40 Op. A.G. 45. 46-47 (1941).

[73] Letter to Hon. John D. Dingell Chairman, House Subcommittee on Oversight and Investigation, Committee on Energy and Commerce, from Attorney General William French Smith, dated November 30, 1982, *reprinted in* H. Rept. No. 97-968, *supra*, at 37-38.

[74] Hearings, *supra* note 62, at __.

[75] See discussion of case law, *supra* at notes 3-15, and accompanying text.

[76] *Hutcheson v. United States,* 369 U.S. 599, 617 (1962).

[77] 369 U.S. at n. 16.

[78] *Sinclair v. United States,* 279 U.S. 263, 294 (1929).

[79] See e.g., *Delaney v. United States,* 199 F.2d 107 (1st Cir. 1952); *United States v. Mitchell,* 372 F.Supp. 1259, 1261 (S.D.N.Y. 1973). For discussion of issues in addition to prejudicial publicity that have been raised in regard to concurrent congressional and judicial proceedings, including allegations of violation of due process, see, Contempt of Congress, H.R. Rpt. No. 97-968, 97th Cong., 2d Sess. 58 (1982).

[80] 199 F.2d 107, 114 (1st Cir. 1952). The court did not fault the committee for holding public hearings, stating that if closed hearings were rejected "because the legislative committee deemed that an open hearing at that time was required by overriding considerations of public interest, then the committee was of course free to go ahead with its hearing, merely accepting the consequence that the trial of Delaney on the pending indictment might have to be delayed." 199 F.2d at 114-5. It reversed Delaney's conviction because the trial court had denied his motion for a continuance until after the publicity generated by the hearing, at which Delaney and other trial witnesses were asked to testify, subsided. See also, *Hutcheson v. United States,* 369 U.S. 599, 613 (1962)(upholding contempt conviction of person who refused to answer committee questions relating to activities for which he had been indicted by a state grand jury, citing *Delaney*)

[81] 199 F.2d at 115.

[82] See, *Silverthorne v. United States,* 400 F.2d 627 (9th Cir. 1968), *cert. denied,* 400 U.S. 102 (1971)(claim of prejudicial pretrial publicity rejected because committee hearings occurred five months prior to indictment); *Beck v. Washington*, 369 U.S. 541, 544 (1962)(hearing occurred a year before trial); *United States v. Haldeman*, 559 F.2d 31, 63 (D.C. Cir. 1976), *cert. denied,* 433 U.S. 933 (1977); *United States v. Ehrlichman,* 546 F.2d 910, 917 (D.C. Cir. 1976), *cert. denied,* 429 U.S. 1120 (1977); *United States* v. *Romano*, 583 F. 2d. 1, 4 (1st Cir. 1978) (Senate Committee determined not to heed warnings from DOJ that insistence on defendant's testimony would threaten or absolutely bar future prosecutions but conviction was nonetheless upheld); *United States v. Mitchell,* 372 F. Supp. 1239, 1261 (S.D.N.Y. 1973)(post-indictment Senate hearing but court held that lapse of time and efforts of committee to avoid questions relating to indictment diminished possibility of prejudice); *United States v. Mesarosh*, 223 F.2d 449 (3rd

Cir. 1955)(hearing only incidentally connected with trial and occurred after jury selected).

[83] See, e.g., *Pillsbury Co. v. FTC,* 354 F.2d 952 5th Cir. (1968).

[84] See e.g., *ATX, Inc. v. Department of Transportation* 41 F.3d 1522 (D.C. Cir. 1994); *State of California v. FERC,* 966 F.2d 154 (9th Cir. 1992); *Peter Kiewet Sons' v. U.S. Army Corps of Engineers,* 714 F.2d 163 (D.C. Cir. 1983); *Gulf Oil Corp. v. FPC,* 563 F.2d 588 (3d Cir. 1977), *cert. denied,* 434 U.S. 1062 (1978); *United States v. Armada Petroleum Corp.,* 562 F.Supp 43 (S.D. Tex. 1982). See also, Morton Rosenberg and Jack Maskell, Congressional Intervention in the Administrative Process: Legal and Ethical Considerations," CRS Report RL32113, September 25, 2003.

[85] Lawrence E. Walsh, "The Independent Counsel and the Separation of Powers," 25 Hous. L. Rev. 1, 9 (1988).

[86] 487 U.S. 654 (1988).

[87] *Id.* at 691-92.

[88] *Id.* at 694.

[89] 9 F.3d 743 (9th Cir. 1993).

[90] 9 F.3d at 751 (emphasis supplied). See also, *Vermont Agency of National Resources* v. *U.S. ex. rel. Stevens*, 529 U.S. 765(2000)(holding that *qui tam* relators meet Article III standing requirements).

[91] *Nixon v. Administration of General Services*, 433 U.S. 425,433 (1977); *Commodity Futures Trading Commission v. Schor*, 487 U.S. 833, 851 (1986); *Morrison v. Olson*, 487 U.S. 654, 693-96 (1988).

[92] *U.S. v. Nixon,* 418 U.S. 683, 705-706, 711-712 (1974).

[93] *Gulf Oil Corp. v. FPC,* 563 F.2d 588, 610 (3d Cir. 1977).

[94] For an in-depth discussion of the *Nixon* and post-Watergate case law, see "Presidential Claims of Executive Privilege: History, Law, Practice and Recent Developments," CRS Report RL30319, 2-9, by Morton Rosenberg.

[95] 121 F.3d 729 (D.C. Cir. 1997).

[96] 365 F.3d 1108 (D.C. Cir. 2004).

[97] Neither case, however, involved congressional access to information.

[98] 121 F.3d 729 (D.C. Cir. 1997).

[99] 121 F.3d at 745, 746; see also *id.* at 737-738 ("[W]here there is reason to believe the documents sought may shed light on government misconduct, the [deliberative process] privilege is routinely denied on the grounds that shielding internal government deliberations in this context does not serve 'the public interest in honest, effective government'").

[100] *Id.* at 745, 752. See also *id.* at 753 ("...these communications nonetheless are ultimately connected with presidential decisionmaking").

[101] *Id.* at 754. See also *id.* at 757.

[102] In contrast, the deliberative process privilege does not protect documents that simply state or explain a decision the government has already made or material that is purely factual, unless the material is inextricably intertwined with the deliberative portions of the materials so that disclosure would effectively reveal the deliberations. 121 F.3d at 737.

[103] *Id.* at 745.

[104] *Id.* at 752.

[105] *Id.*

[106] *Id.* (footnote omitted).

[107] *Id.* at 752.

[108] *Id.* at 752-53.

[109] See, e.g., Kendall ex rel. Stokes v. United States, 37 U.S. (12 Pet.) 522, 612-613 (1838); *Youngstown Sheet and Tube Co. v. Sawyer,* 343 U.S. 579, 587 (1952); *Myers v. United States,* 272 U.S. 52, 177 (1926)(Holmes, J., dissenting); *National Treasury Employees Union v. Nixon,* 492 F.2d 587, 604 (D.C. Cir. (1974): *Biodiversity Associates, et al* v. *Cables*, 357 F. 3d. 1152, 1161-63(10th Cir. 2004)("[W]hen Congress is exercising its own powers with respect to matters of public rights, the executive role of 'tak[ing] Care that the Laws be faithfully executed,' U.S. Const. Art. II, §3, is entirely derivative of the laws passed by Congress, and Congress may be as specific in its instruction to the executive as it wishes.").

[110] 418 U.S. 683 (1974).

[111] *Id.* at 748.

[112] *Id.* at 750.

[113] *Id.* at 752.

[114] 365 F.3d 1108 (D.C. Cir. 2004). The panel split 2-1, with Judge Rogers writing for the majority and Judge Randolph dissenting.

[115] The President has delegated the formal process of review and recommendation of his pardon authority to the Attorney General who in turn has delegated it to the Deputy Attorney General. The Deputy Attorney General oversees the work of the Office of the Pardon Attorney.

[116] 365 F.3d at 1109-12.

[117] *Id.* at 1112, 1114, 1123.

[118] *Id.* at 1114.

[119] *Id.* at 1117.

[120] *Id.* at 1121. See also *Id.* at 1122.

[121] *Id.* at 1116.

[122] *Id.* at 1116, 1117.

[123] *Id.* at 1118-24.

[124] 5 U.S.C. 553(b)(5)(1994).

[125] 5 U.S.C. 552 d).

[126] 613 F. 2d 1151 (D.C. Cir. 1979).

[127] 613 F. 2d at 1155-56, 1158.

[128] 421 U.S. 132 (1975).

[129] 421 U.S. at 161 (emphasis in original).

[130] *McGrain v. Daugherty,* 272 U.S. 135, 175 (1927).

[131] 365 F. 3d. at 1123.

[132] Other memoranda and documents from the Department were reviewed by the subcommittee and kept in its confidential files, for example, a letter of instruction from the Attorney General to the Department attorney that had been sent to St. Louis. *Id.* at 890. In addition, the district court judge that had convened the grand jury gave the subcommittee permission to use the notes of the U .S. Attorney in St. Louis and of one of the grand jurors, with all names deleted. *Id.* The judge also submitted a deposition to the subcommittee about the Department's interference with the grand jury. *Id.* at 891-93.

INDEX

A

access, ix, x, 2, 4, 10, 12, 13, 14, 15, 18, 19, 24, 26, 27, 29, 36, 37, 39, 40, 41, 44, 45, 49, 50, 51, 52, 53, 54, 55, 56, 57, 58, 59, 60, 61, 63, 66, 68, 69, 70, 71, 73, 80
accommodation, 24, 30, 69
administration, 1, 3, 5, 6, 7, 11, 24, 27, 45, 46, 51, 67
agent, 16, 21, 53, 65, 67, 68
alternatives, 34
ambassadors, 33, 40
appendix, 4, 43
argument, 35, 37, 38
arrest, 10, 44
assessment, 3
attention, 73
Attorney General, x, 3, 6, 10, 11, 13, 14, 15, 16, 18, 20, 23, 24, 27, 28, 34, 35, 36, 43, 44, 45, 46, 47, 48, 49, 50, 51, 53, 54, 55, 56, 57, 60, 61, 62, 63, 64, 65, 67, 69, 70, 73, 75, 78, 81, 82
authority, 5, 6, 7, 10, 26, 29, 32, 33, 34, 36, 37, 39, 40, 41, 46, 81
autonomy, 12
availability, 73

B

behavior, 1
benefits, 56
brutality, 49
bureaucracy, 33

C

caliber, 34
California, 80
campaigns, 68
case law, x, 3, 79, 80
case study, 19
certification, 13, 15, 59, 62
chain of command, 31, 36
Chief of Staff, 73, 74
CIA, 64
civil rights, 49
commander-in-chief, 33
Committee on the Judiciary, 43, 47, 54, 62, 74, 78
common law, 2, 4, 9, 31, 37
community, 52
compliance, 1, 11, 16, 65, 69
components, 55
conception, 25

confidentiality, 24, 29, 31, 32, 34, 57
conflict, 13, 14, 59, 60, 69
conflict of interest, 13, 14, 59, 60, 69
confrontation, 58
Congress, iv, ix, x, 1, 2, 5, 6, 7, 9, 11, 17, 19, 23, 24, 25, 26, 27, 28, 29, 33, 36, 37, 39, 43, 44, 46, 47, 49, 50, 52, 53, 58, 59, 65, 69, 70, 72, 74, 76, 77, 79, 81
congressional budget, ix, 1
consent, 49, 50, 51, 70
conspiracy, 72, 78
Constitution, x, 1, 5, 24, 34, 40
constraints, 5
consumer protection, 33
control, 11, 28, 45, 66, 67, 68
conviction, 7, 46, 56, 71, 79
corruption, 6, 9, 10, 18, 25, 45, 48, 58, 70
costs, 48, 56
counsel, 15, 28, 47, 57, 61, 69
coupling, 37
Court of Appeals, 28
coverage, 36
crime, 25
criminal activity, 28
criminal statutes, 63
criminality, 53
CRS, 74, 75, 80
culture, 16, 65

D

danger, 6, 24, 26
death, 20
decisions, 5, 6, 17, 18, 25, 29, 30, 40, 65, 70, 72
defendants, 26, 50
demand, 29, 30
denial, 57, 66
Department of Energy, 16, 53, 64
Department of Justice, i, iii, iv, vii, ix, x, 2, 6, 10, 13, 16, 18, 20, 30, 34, 39, 43, 44, 46, 47, 48, 49, 50, 51, 52, 55, 59, 64, 65, 66, 71, 75, 76, 77
Department of the Interior, 10, 44
deposition, 82
destruction, 68
disclosure, x, 2, 3, 7, 10, 11, 18, 23, 34, 38, 39, 46, 51, 56, 70, 71, 81
disposition, 54, 62
District of Columbia, 13, 14, 30, 34, 59, 60
division, 14, 60
draft, 62, 68
due process, 25, 79
duties, 1, 3, 6, 27, 40, 46, 56

E

election, 68
emotional distress, 72, 78
employees, ix, x, 3, 9, 14, 17, 18, 30, 38, 39, 43, 51, 61, 62, 65, 71, 72
Energy and Commerce Committee, 12
engagement, 20
environmental policy, 33
Environmental Protection Agency, 11, 16, 58, 59, 65, 66, 76
EPA, viii, 11, 12, 13, 14, 15, 16, 23, 58, 59, 60, 61, 65, 66, 76
evidence, 7, 15, 19, 31, 38, 46, 47, 48, 53, 61, 64, 68, 72
excuse, 7, 46
execution, 3
Executive Branch, 6, 14, 18, 28, 29, 30, 58, 60, 71
executive function, 27, 29
executive functions, 29
exercise, 23, 27, 28, 32, 34, 36, 38
exposure, 25

F

failure, 9, 10, 19, 44, 47, 53, 55, 71, 73, 78

faith, 30
FBI, vii, viii, ix, x, 2, 9, 15, 16, 17, 18, 19, 20, 24, 49, 51, 52, 53, 55, 56, 57, 58, 62, 64, 65, 66, 68, 69, 70, 71, 72, 75, 77
fear(s), 35, 38, 56
Federal Bureau of Investigation, 18, 20, 52, 70
federal law, 20
field agents, x
finance, 68, 69
foreign affairs, 27
fraud, 1, 5, 27, 37, 47, 48
freedom, 32
fuel, 53

G

GAO, 52, 53
General Accounting Office, 52
goals, ix, 1, 2, 10, 44
government, ix, 1, 2, 3, 5, 7, 16, 18, 23, 24, 27, 29, 31, 32, 33, 36, 37, 41, 43, 46, 47, 54, 64, 65, 71, 72, 78, 80, 81
grand jury, 13, 14, 16, 18, 31, 47, 56, 59, 60, 62, 65, 70, 79, 82
grants, 34
groups, 52
guidance, 63
guidelines, 10, 53, 56
guilty, 62

H

House, x, 3, 11, 12, 13, 16, 17, 24, 31, 32, 36, 40, 43, 46, 49, 51, 52, 53, 55, 56, 58, 59, 62, 63, 64, 66, 69, 70, 71, 72, 73, 74, 76, 77, 78

I

Idaho, 20, 78
identity, 23, 62
immunity, 73
impeachment, ix, 1
implementation, ix, 1, 2
in situ, 25
individual rights, 1
industry, 49, 53
inefficiency, 6, 27
injury, iv
inspectors, 20
institutional change, 20
instruction, 17, 66, 81, 82
integrity, ix, x, 2, 24, 52
intelligence, 51, 52, 53, 54, 55
Intelligence Committee, 55
interference, 2, 23, 48, 82
interview, 14, 16, 61, 65, 66
Iran, viii, ix, x, 2, 9, 27, 63
Iran-Contra, viii, ix, x, 2, 9, 27, 63

J

judgment, 6
Judiciary, 13, 20, 49, 52, 53, 54, 58, 59, 62, 67, 72, 74, 76
Judiciary Committee, 13, 20, 49, 52, 53, 59, 62, 67, 72, 74
juries, 10, 19, 71
jurisdiction, x, 3, 39
justice, 18, 24, 48, 70

K

killing, 20

L

labor, 33
labor relations, 33
land, 7, 46
law enforcement, ix, x, 2, 3, 11, 17, 19, 23, 24, 28, 29, 39, 40, 55, 70, 72
laws, 1, 3, 5, 7, 23, 26, 28, 29, 33, 39, 46, 47, 68, 81

lead, 78
Legal Expense Trust, 68
legislation, ix, 1, 2, 6, 10, 25, 39, 46, 58
Libya, viii, 54
likelihood, 30
limitation, 33, 35, 73
line attorneys,, x
litigation, 9, 11, 24, 25, 41, 63, 75

M

malfeasance, 9
management, 29, 63
management practices, 63
Massachusetts, 71, 78
military, 27
money, 63, 68
motion, 31, 79
murder, 18, 70

N

national security, 27
National Security Council, 64
neglect, 6, 46
negligence, 72, 78
negotiating, 40
negotiation, 11, 12, 49, 75
New England, 19, 70, 71, 72, 77
New Mexico, 73
New York, iii, v, 49
nuclear weapons, 16, 64

O

obligation, 33
obstruction, 19, 72
oil, 10, 44, 49, 53
openness, 36
organizations, 5
oversight, ix, 1, 3, 4, 5, 6, 9, 17, 19, 26, 27, 28, 29, 30, 37, 38, 39, 40, 52

P

performance, x, 1, 3, 38
permit, 14, 56, 57, 58, 61
personal, 16, 35, 56, 65
Petroleum, 80
plutonium, 16, 65
polarization, 24
police, 49
poor, 1
posture, 67
power, 1, 2, 5, 7, 9, 18, 25, 26, 28, 29, 33, 34, 36, 39, 40, 46, 55, 70
predicate, 15, 62
prejudice, 23, 24, 25, 26, 63, 79
President Bush, 17, 71, 77
President Clinton, 31, 34, 68
pressure, 26
privacy, 52
probability, 38
probe, x, 3, 6, 66
production, 5, 11, 16, 45, 58, 63, 65
profits, 16, 65
program, 1, 66
promote, 29
proposition, 25
public interest, 24, 25, 35, 38, 39, 51, 79, 80
public policy, ix, 1, 2, 3, 39, 40

Q

questioning, 10, 26, 44, 47, 56

R

range, 10, 44, 47
reading, 33, 34
reasoning, 25, 38
recognition, 32, 35
recollection, 17, 66
recovery, 16, 65
regional, 9

regulations, 68
relationship, 66, 68
Republican, 68
reserves, 10, 44
resistance, 20, 66
resolution, 2, 17, 74
rigidity, 18, 71
risk, 32, 35

S

safety, 33
sales, 11, 45
scandal, 10, 44, 63, 64
scores, 10, 44
search, 68
security, 2, 53
Senate, 6, 7, 10, 20, 43, 44, 45, 46, 51, 52, 54, 55, 58, 63, 67, 68, 72, 73, 75, 78, 79
sensitivity, 2, 54
separation, 18, 28, 31, 70
separation of powers, 28, 31
September 11, 70
series, 6, 14, 60, 63
sharing, 69
species, 37
St. Clair expedition, ix
St. Louis, 47, 82
stages, 12, 68
statute of limitations, 10, 44
statutes, 5, 29, 32, 49
subpoena, x, 3, 6, 12, 16, 17, 31, 45, 58, 65, 66, 67, 69, 70, 73
summaries, 4, 9, 16, 19, 43, 53, 55, 65, 71
Superfund, vii, 11, 12, 23
supervision, 1, 28, 56
supervisor, 68
supply, 2, 13, 43, 54, 60, 74
Supreme Court, x, 3, 5, 6, 7, 9, 24, 27, 29, 38, 39, 40, 45, 46
surveillance, 10, 44

T

Take Care" clause, x
Teapot Dome, ix
telephone, 47, 49
terrorist attack, 70
threat, 12
threshold, x, 3, 31
time, 2, 12, 14, 17, 18, 19, 26, 36, 44, 47, 51, 53, 54, 60, 66, 67, 68, 69, 70, 72, 79
time frame, 54
top management, 67
transcripts, 47, 49, 56, 73
treaties, 33, 40
trial, 23, 25, 26, 53, 78, 79
triggers, 16, 65

U

United Nations, 48
United States, iv, viii, ix, x, 2, 5, 7, 9, 13, 14, 16, 20, 25, 28, 34, 39, 44, 46, 49, 58, 59, 60, 65, 67, 71, 72, 75, 76, 77, 78, 79, 80, 81

V

validity, x, 3, 28
venue, 25
Vermont, 80

W

Washington, 66, 67, 72, 78, 79
Watergate,, ix
White House, 12, 18, 31, 32, 35, 36, 40, 55, 68, 71, 73, 74
Whitewater,, ix
witnesses, 10, 11, 16, 17, 19, 23, 25, 45, 48, 49, 52, 55, 56, 62, 65, 66, 73, 79
workplace, 33

writing, 74, 81
wrongdoing, x, 3, 13, 20, 25, 59

Y

yield, 39